The Green Guide to SCOTLAND

John Button

Green Print
1990

Other Green Guides in this series:
The Green Guide to England (John Button)
The Green Guide to France (Mary Davis)

Other books by John Button:
A Dictionary of Green Ideas (Routledge, 1987)
How To Be Green (Century, 1989)
The New Green Pages (Optima, April 1990)

Acknowledgements

As with *The Green Guide to England*, this guide relies heavily on the help and research of many other people. Thank you to everybody who helped in the collection of material for the Scottish volume: the regional tourist board information officers, Elliott Blaauew, Chris Bunyan, Liz and Brian Chaplin, Chris Church, Chloë Dear, Margaret Elphinstone, Brian Fleming, Marianna Lines, Sue Mellis, Marion Paul, Rosemary Turnbull, Linda Wilson and Helen Witchall. As usual, special thanks to Eric Back for proofreading. The Victorian illustrations are from an 1880 edition of *Black's Picturesque Tourist in Scotland*.

ISBN 1 85425 029 9

First published 1990 by Green Print,
an imprint of The Merlin Press Ltd,
10 Malden Road, London NW5 3HR (Tel: 0(7)1 267 3399)

Set in Palatino by the author and Saxon Printing Ltd

Printed in Great Britain by Biddles Ltd, Guildford, on 100% recycled paper

Contents

How to use this book

Just like *The Green Guide to England*, *The Green Guide to Scotland* is set out much like other guidebooks, taking you region by region around the country and suggesting interesting places you might like to visit. What sets it apart from other guidebooks is its approach to tourism, and the sorts of things it recommends you to do and see during your travels.

The first chapter asks what travelling is all about and why we do it at all. It also looks at what tourism does to places and communities. The next three chapters explore what Scotland has to offer to the visitor who travels with open eyes and an open mind. Then there is an introduction to the different elements of the green movement in Scotland, and a practical chapter dealing with things like food, money, travel and contacts.

The main part of *The Green Guide to Scotland* is the regional sections, where for convenience the forty-odd tourist board areas have been divided into ten regions: the maps at the section openings show which areas are covered by which boards. After a short introduction to the region, there is a description and directory, under various headings, for each major urban area in the region, followed by a similar directory section for the region as a whole.

The aim of *The Green Guide to Scotland* is to include as many places as possible worth visiting, with enough information for you to be able to find them easily.

As always with books of this kind, we would appreciate feedback. If you come across inaccuracies, or new places that you think should be included in future editions, please write to us at the address on the back of the title page.

The green traveller

If you were to ask most people to describe the ideal place to live, it would be somewhere convenient for all the urban services that we in the late twentieth century have come to expect, somewhere beautiful and secluded and where other people — unless they had been specifically invited — were *not*. 'A front door on Oxford Street and a back door overlooking the Sound of Mull' is how Nan Fairbrother once put it.

Since most of us have neither Oxford Street nor the Sound of Mull within easy reach, we do our best to compromise by making our indoor environment as comfortable as possible, and travelling in order to find the Oxford Streets and Sounds of Mull of this world.

I have always found compromise hard, especially when it concerns a place to live in. To a large extent this is why I have lived in Scotland for the last twenty years, the last several in Galloway — the 'bonnie Gallowa' ' of the Victorian songwriter. You won't find cinemas and concert halls in my home town of Kirkcudbright, but I have within walking distance all the shops I need for everyday things, a head post office, and a bus station offering fairly regular services throughout the region (and a twice-daily coach to London).

The residents of this small Scottish town also have woods and hills to walk in without first having to get in the car, while within half an hour's drive are rocky valleys, sandy beaches and desolate moorland. And though it is being steadily eroded as people buy the centuries-old cottages as second homes, Kirkcudbright is still a community, a place where people greet each other in the street, drop round to visit without first making complex arrangements and don't bother to lock the door when they go shopping.

For me this all begs the question of what travelling is really about, and what the tourist industry does to the places that feature prominently in the guidebooks. In its own small way Kirkcudbright is a tourist town, as you can tell from the bagpipe skirl on summer Thursday evenings and the tartan haggises in the couple of souvenir shops, but it does it with a degree of dignity and on a scale in keeping with its character.

Try forcing your way up Edinburgh's Royal Mile on a summer's afternoon or finding somewhere to park in the Trossachs during a bank holiday, and you will see a different side of Scotland's tourist industry. Unless you actively like exhaust fumes and being hemmed in by crowds of people, you will begin to wonder about the relaxation you came to find on your Scottish holiday.

The stress of travelling has been researched extensively, showing that you are much more likely to be ill or injure yourself while on holiday than at any other time. There are constant claims on your time, money and attention; delays, cancellations and traffic jams; banks which shut before you can reach them and restaurants that won't take your plastic money; cold coffee and dirty toilets. But tourism is not only stressful for the traveller. Think of the people who live on the Royal Mile and what it must be like going out for a pint of milk of an August afternoon.

Then think of the more popular of Scotland's mountain areas. The development of Scotland's premier ski resort in the Cairngorm Mountains has concerned many conservationists, causing the Scottish Countryside Commission to report that 'Over the last thirty years there has been a proliferation of footpaths, particularly where access is easy, and little effort has been put to their repair.' The footpaths on Ben Ledi, one of Scotland's most popular and accessible mountains, are being 'trampled to death' according to a recent contributor to the magazine *Climber and Hill Walker*. The paths on this one mountain alone require an investment of several million pounds in the next decade.

Travellers have been visiting Scotland for centuries, from Suetonius in the third century to Queen Victoria in the nineteenth, but it is only relatively recently that the tourist industry has grown so rapidly that in places it threatens the very things that people come to see. In 1987 nearly 15 million people spent a holiday in Scotland, paying nearly £2 billion for the privilege. Around a million of them visited Edinburgh Castle, a figure exceeded only by the numbers visiting the Winter Gardens in Aberdeen and the Disney-like Magnum Leisure Centre in Irvine.

Can this sort of travelling still be called travelling in any real sense? Surely there is a volume of tourism at which all you can expect to see is other tourists and facilities which have been provided purely for tourists. As John Julius Norwich has written: 'The easier it becomes to travel, the harder it is to be a traveller.'

Holidays are traditionally a time for 'getting away from it all', seeing and learning about new places. But in the economic climate of the latter decades of the twentieth century the primary purpose of tourism is neither relaxation nor education. It is to make money. The seasoned traveller knows that even if you are very careful, clear and assertive, your hard-earned holiday savings will still disappear like snow in summer.

Of course there are many people involved in the tourist industry who see standard of service and customer satisfaction as vitally important, but somebody has to provide the wherewithal to keep castles, cathedrals, footpaths and parks in order, and at a time of public service cutbacks the costs are increasingly being passed on to the 'consumer'.

Thus the last few years have seen a proliferation of wildlife theme parks and heritage centres, alias the 'nature industry' and the 'heritage industry'. At a time of growing green and social awareness, large companies and corporations have been quick to sponsor projects in exchange for having their name and logo on entrance plaques and literature. Luckily the public service tradition dies hard, and there are still many worthwhile things to see in Scotland which you can visit as of right rather than as a privilege.

At its worst, tourism has become a blind quest for a certain kind of bland, carefully-arranged experience. Its consumers no longer make pilgrimages to considered destinations, but instead wander from town to town looking for distraction. The more money that distraction costs, the more pleased are its purveyors (and, strangely enough, are many of its customers too, since having to pay for something seems to imbue it with an intrinsic value).

The experience of travelling is made even more bland by the growth of look-alike tourist facilities: the ubiquitous games arcades, fast food takeaways and plastic souvenir shops. Luckily Scotland has, with a few notable exceptions, escaped the worst excesses of this trend, and further incursions should be resisted at all costs.

Is it still possible to travel with any integrity at all in the last decade of the twentieth century, or does the environmental and social damage we do negate any benefits we might gain from it? Travelling, even in an aware way with our eyes and minds wide open, still uses scarce resources and adds to the pressure upon an already overloaded environment, but it is also the only way to experience at first hand places and cultures which are different from our own.

The first question that any potential green traveller should have uppermost when considering any journey is: 'Is my journey really necessary?' Why do you want to get away? What is it that you need to do somewhere other than here? It is too easy to believe that only somewhere else will provide you with what you need, and always having somewhere else to go to is the perfect excuse for not making here a pleasanter place in which to spend your time. And how much of your holidays do you spend wishing that you were at home?

The second important consideration for the green traveller is to do with respect, a vital aspect of any green lifestyle. Are you respecting the landscape and the culture of the places you visit, or is what you are doing damaging them? Even in a small country like Scotland there is an enormous diversity of landscape and culture, and the ecological principle of diversity guaranteeing sustainability operates in the social sphere just as it does in the environmental.

This means that the green traveller will take a real interest in places and people, treating them as the unique and important elements that they are of the Scottish scene. They will notice where they are, how that place differs from other places, and what makes it tick. They will ask intelligent questions rather than laying down the law. They will buy the products of local manufacturers and craftspeople rather than plastic imports and shrinkwrapped long-life foods.

The green traveller knows that everywhere in the world the environment is under threat from human activities, and that the pressure of tourism is yet another such pressure. Looking after the environment must always take priority, and although guidelines like the Country Code provide a basis, it is important to remember that every decision you take has environmental consequences. The green traveller, for example, would never drop litter; they would also try to create as little waste as possible in the first place. They wouldn't disturb wildlife or leave a gate open, but they would also understand the need to respect the needs of all living things.

But, as I said at the beginning of *The Green Guide to England*, there is a terrible temptation to believe that if you are being a 'good green traveller' then that somehow makes you a better person than the hordes of non-green travellers. Don't kid yourself. All travellers are consumers, and nearly all travelling involves more consumption than staying at home.

The question 'Is your journey really necessary?' raises a number of other questions. Until relatively recently very few people 'went away' for their infrequent 'holydays'. They spent them in their own communities, enjoying time together and acknowledging the natural cycles and rhythms which provided them with a living. Most traditional societies in the world would have difficulty understanding what a holiday — in the Western sense — is. Only recently have we been forced into believing that a holiday must involve a long and often arduous journey, a strange and sometimes bewildering setting, a solitary patch on a faraway beach and the stress of getting to know new people.

More than anything else it is our need to escape that has created tourism, but once we have discovered that the conventional jetaway escape only fulfils some of our needs we might look at other ways of changing our lives. If we had more control over every aspect of our lives and surroundings — a very green idea — then we would stand a much better chance of making here the place where we would choose to spend most of our time. Then on the few occasions when we actively chose to travel we could say, like my Auntie Dorothy, 'Well, we saw a lot of wonderful things, but it *was* nice to get home again.'

What Scotland has to offer

There can be few countries in the world where fact and fiction, reality and imagination, natural wonder and magical myth, are so entwined and indistinguishable as in Scotland. The fifteen million people who come to visit every year, bringing with them more than 6% of Scotland's total income, have their own individual quests, yet few come without a hint of an expectation of Scotland as the land of kilts, bagpipes, tartans, whisky, golf, heather moors, mist, lochs and monsters.

And because Scotland is largely dependent upon perpetuating this important source of income, it willingly perpetuates those things which bring the tourists, forcing itself to believe that clan tartans and the skirl of the pipes indeed belong to their nation's misty and ancient past. Never mind that tartan was invented only in 1832, and the pipes even later.

Because of their unique and chequered history, first as a loose amalgam of very different cultures and then as partners in the unequal union with England, Scots have always had to work hard to maintain a Scottish identity. The temptation to compare Scotland with England, even by Scottish writers, is overwhelming, but when for most purposes the two countries are now one and Scotland has clearly benefited less from the link, nobody can blame Scots for sometimes feeling hard done by.

Yet in many ways Scotland is still very different from the rest of the United Kingdom, retaining its own church, law courts, educational system, language, literature and banknotes. And most Scots are proud of most of their heritage, even though the traditional toast of 'Here's tae us; wha's lik' us; gey few an' they're a' deid' may seem a little melodramatic.

One thing the English can never take from the Scots (though the sale of estates and country cottages to incomers is a contentious issue) is the country's often breathtaking scenery. Even in the middle of a Scottish city the hills and lochs are close at hand. The residents of Edinburgh are only a bus ride from the Pentland Hills and Arthur's Seat, while the knife-edge of the Campsies broods over Glasgow's northern suburbs.

As an 1847 gazetteer of Scotland flamboyantly explains: 'So wondrously diverse is the surface of Scotland that each of all its parishes has some distinctive features of its own, and each of very many offers to the painter entire groups, sometimes multitudinous clusters, of scenes which are rich in the peculiarities of their respective elements.' Many visitors to Scotland are surprised how large and diverse the country is. Borderers and Lewis islanders have about as much and as little in common with each other as do the inhabitants of Kent and central Wales. Shetland is further from Edinburgh than Cornwall is from London.

Most historians agree that while Scotland was the birthplace of many a world-changing technology, from telephones to antiseptics, its most potent and influential export has been its people. More than 15 million people worldwide claim descent from Scots who have emigrated in the last 150 years (the population of Scotland is only 5 million today). Between 1901 and 1961 alone, nearly 1½ million Scots left their native land, two thirds of the natural increase in that period. No other European country has ever lost such a high proportion of her people.

And many of those that now come to visit Scotland claim descent from these more or less willing emigrants. Civic dignitaries from New Zealand, government ministers from Australia, families called Mackay with a pronounced Texan drawl and young Canadians learning Gaelic all come to find their ancestral homes and their clan tartans.

After many centuries of Scottish nationhood centred on the castles of Stirling, Dunfermline and Edinburgh, since the Union of 1707 Scotland has been peripheral to the larger state of which it now forms part. Though resourceful, intelligent and inventive, Scots have suffered increasingly from economic and social policies which have not taken the real needs of people and environment into account. Interwar 'planning' led many of Scotland's traditional heavy industries into terminal decline, while recent policies have done much the same for hosiery, papermaking and transport industries. Large sums of money pumped into urban Scotland for high-rise housing and destructive road-building left a legacy of poverty and dereliction, especially in the Glasgow area.

This is a side of Scotland's heritage that few guidebooks will dwell upon, but along with ageing nuclear power stations and a massive military presence it is just as important an aspect of the country as the mountains and beaches preferred by other guides. The intelligent traveller knows this, and wants to hear about every aspect of the real Scotland.

Despite the massive scale of the problems, there have been concerted efforts in recent years to make urban (and rural) Scotland a more attractive and fulfilling place to live and work. Though lack of money is often a problem, one thing which Scots have in abundance is community spirit, and community projects in some of the country's most deprived areas are showing what can be achieved when people's real needs are taken into account. From the renovation of Glasgow tower blocks to the provision of rural co-operatives in the Western Isles, the greening of Scotland is under way.

Wherever you are in Scotland you will not be far from a tourist information centre and a public library — even most small towns have both. From the tourist information centre you will be able to collect a sheaf of useful information (though remember to save paper by taking only what you really need!), and you will usually find the staff extremely helpful. The public library will have a collection of books and pamphlets about the local area, some of which you may be able to borrow if you are staying in the area for a few days. There will also be a noticeboard giving details of forthcoming events.

The Scottish Tourist Board (23 Ravelston Terrace, Edinburgh EH4 3EU; Tel: 031 332 2433) is the statutory body promoting tourism in Scotland. They will be happy to provide general information, and there are departments which deal specifically with foreign visitors with particular interests, and with research enquiries. Their general booklet, *Scotland: where to go and what to see*, is published in eight languages.

Preliminary enquiries from overseas can usually be dealt with by British Tourist Authority (BTA) offices in your own country — there are offices in 21 countries, including four in the USA (Chicago, Dallas, Los Angeles and New York). Tourism in Scotland is administered by 36 area tourist boards; these are the best places from which to request more detailed information. The BTA produces annually a complete list of all tourist information centres in Britain; this is available free on request. The addresses of each of the area tourist boards will be found in the appropriate regional sections later in the book.

Very many guidebooks have been written about Scotland, but few give a good overall impression of what today's Scotland is really like. This is partly because many writers of guidebooks to Scotland are not Scottish, partly because everybody's Scotland is different, partly because guidebooks tend to include only what they think their readers want to hear, and partly because the variety of Scottish landscape and culture is difficult to capture within the covers of a single book.

Of the single-volume guides to Scotland it is hard to pick out one good one, but if forced I would choose the *Times Bartholemew Guide to Scotland*, because as well as being up to date it includes some interesting background reading. If you plan to spend some time in Scotland, then the two New Shell Guides, *Northern Scotland and the Islands* by Francis Thompson and *The Lowlands and Borders of Scotland* by Roddy Martine, are well-written and good value. All you really need to begin with, though, is a good map, and here the Scottish Tourist Board's *Touring Map* is excellent, showing everything from sandy beaches to castles and parks.

If you want a more personal and in-depth exploration of Scotland today, some titles you might look out for are *Scotland 2000: Eight Views on the State of the Nation* (BBC, 1987) and Kenneth Roy's accurate and acerbic *Travels in a Small Country* (Carrick, 1987). Bookshops in Scotland, especially the larger ones like Waterstone's or Thin's in Edinburgh and John Smith's in Glasgow, carry a comprehensive selection of books about Scotland, and offer a mail order service.

The rest of this chapter is written primarily for overseas visitors to Scotland, and tries to answer three of the most important questions that anyone planning a holiday in Scotland will ask first:

— Where should I go?
— When should I go?
— How much detailed arranging should I do beforehand?

What Scotland has to offer

Do remember that — contrary to what you may be led to believe — Scotland is a fairly large country rather than merely a speck on the European map. Therefore do not try to do too much in one visit; you will only tire yourself out and put both the human and wildlife populations of the country at risk as you rush around from attraction to attraction.

Where you decide to go will depend very much upon your interests, what you have heard about and where you have been before, and where your Scottish friends and acquaintances live. If I were visiting Scotland for the first time and had a couple of weeks to spend travelling around the country, I would certainly want to spend time in both Edinburgh and Glasgow (two or three days in each, including time to explore the surrounding country-side); otherwise I would avoid the main tourist traps, especially in high summer. I would want to spend several days walking in the hills, would do my best to get to some of Scotland's farther-flung islands, and would arrange to visit maybe half a dozen places and projects which particularly interested me — a community housing project, a craft village, an organic farm. One way of overcoming the anonymity (and potential anomie) of travelling is to join a short course or workshop where you can learn new skills and meet like-minded people; at least it gives you a few days in one place to catch up with your sleep and your washing.

I'm afraid that almost everything they say about Scotland's weather is true; it is extremely fickle. A holiday in the height of summer can be unstintingly wet and windy, while a sunny week in April or October can make for an unforgettable stay. Because the Scottish landscape is so varied, conditions can even change within the course of a couple of dozen miles. I have travelled through torrential rain, thick mist and bright sunshine during a two-hour journey from Galloway to Edinburgh. You will therefore need to take with you the necessary gear for rain, cold and heat. Although you will be able to find peace and solitude at any time of year if you choose your places carefully, the better-known resorts do fill up quite noticeably during the school summer holidays: these are from early July to late August in Scotland, and late July to early September in England, whence more than half of Scotland's British-based tourists originate.

There is always a tendency to try to do too much while on holiday, and if you are not careful you will end up ill and exhausted. Only very rarely will it prove difficult to find somewhere to stay wherever you are in Scotland, even in August, so you don't need to plan your trip in great detail. Overplanning can even be counterproductive, since it leaves no space for chance encounters and unforeseen invitations. Do book ahead when you know what you want to do, especially for popular places and events like festival performances, but leave plenty of gaps too. Some American friends of mine were very glad they hadn't made too many advance plans when they met, quite by chance, some distantly-related cousins and were invited to join a weekend party at a beautifully-restored Borders tower house.

The natural landscape

Most Scots would agree that their country is both beautiful and unique, a valuable natural asset that must be conserved for future generations of humans and wildlife alike. Yet the threats to the natural environment are ever-present, and though the tide of unawareness now seems to be on the turn, there can be few societies which take so little care of the land which sustains it. From the acidification of the hills by endless conifer planting to the ever-present threat of nuclear waste dumping, the Scottish landscape — sometimes chronically and sometimes subtly — is under attack.

Much of the reason for this is that fewer than 3% of Scots now work on the land: four out of five live in a city or town. Many of those who live in the countryside commute to work in urban areas, while most depend on nearby towns for shopping and services. Because most Scots have so few links with the ground under their feet, they often have little idea of what is being done to it in the name of progress. The 'natural landscape' in many parts of Scotland is often far from what nature would create if left entirely to its own devices, being the result of centuries of complex interaction between natural processes and human influences.

On the other hand, Scotland contains large areas where the human population is very thin on the ground. Though far from their truly natural state when compared with the Siberian tundra or the Amazon rainforest, the North-West Highlands and the

Cairngorms are the closest areas in Britain akin to wilderness. As a result of the activities of the managers of sheep, grouse and softwood trees these areas are rarely without evidence of human activity, but there are places, especially at high altitudes, where such activity has had a negligible effect on the landscape.

And it is a landscape which we have come to understand to a large extent through the researches and insights of a number of renowned Scottish pioneers in natural history, people of the stature of Hugh Miller, John Muir and Archibald Geikie.

Geology

Compared with the complex geology of England, the rocks of Scotland are — with some exceptions — relatively easy to understand. Also when compared with the England, most of Scotland's rocks are very old. The hard Lewisian gneiss found in the Outer Hebrides is one of the most ancient rocks in the world.

While the overall geological pattern of Scotland is one of broad bands of similar rocks divided by massive faults running from south-west to north-east, the western Highlands have been carved from some of the most complex geological structures in the world, where late volcanic activity has crumpled and changed the structure of the surrounding rocks. This has made the region a classic area for the study of both geology and scenery.

If you are interested in geology, your visit to Scotland should include the Geology Floor of the Royal Museum of Scotland in Edinburgh, where you will find a comprehensive collection of minerals and interesting displays explaining many aspects of Scottish geology and landscape. The Geological Survey publishes geological maps of Scotland. These are available for most of Scotland at two scales: 1:250,000 and 1/50,000. The larger-scale maps are sometimes available in two versions, one showing the underlying rock formations ('solid'), the other showing what is to be found at the land surface ('drift'); in less geologically complex areas both are shown on the same sheet.

Though there have been many more recent books on the geology of Scotland, notably (for the interested amateur) J.B. Whittow's *Geology and Scenery in Scotland* (Penguin, 1977), it is worth looking in a library for Sir Archibald Geikie's *Scenery of Scotland*, published in 1901, which in words and clear engravings explains the intricacies of the Scottish landscape as well as any more recent volume.

Landforms

Geomorphology is the study of different landforms and how they have come to be the way they are. It is to a very large extent the twin influences of glaciation during the last great ice age and the power of the sea which have formed the most dramatic elements of the Scottish landscape, such as the impressive 'crag and tail' outcrop which provides the setting for Edinburgh castle and the majestic sea stack of the Old Man of Hoy in Orkney. It is ice that has created the vast areas of bare deeply-scored rock in the western Highlands and the distinctive drumlin scenery of Tweedsdale in the Borders, while the sea has carved caves, islands, and some of the highest cliffs in Europe. The wind too has played its part, creating east of Inverness one of the largest dune areas in Europe, the Culbin Sands.

A good introduction to geomorphology in Britain is a book called *Landshapes* (David and Charles, 1988, £14.95), a collection of case studies by some of Britain's leading geomorphologists. For Scotland in particular, Whittow's *Geology and Scenery in Scotland* (see under 'Geology') is good, but J.B. Sissons's *The Evolution of Scotland's Scenery* (Oliver and Boyd, 1967) is even better — both are now unfortunately out of print.

Rivers and seas

In a country with such a wet climate as Scotland, streams and rivers are an important and ever-present part of the landscape. They are usually too cold to swim in, though the clear water of a mountain stream can be most welcome to a thirsty and footsore summer hiker.

There is dramatic river scenery to be explored in Scotland, as at the Falls of Clyde near New Lanark or the Tummel at the Queen's View near Pitlochry. But many of Scotland's rivers are also threatened with pollution from industrial and agricultural malpractice: the Tweed and the Clyde have recently been the subject of large-scale pollution incidents.

Detailed, yet very readable, information about the current state of water quality in Scotland's rivers is included in a collection of essays, edited by Edward Goldsmith and Nicholas Hildyard, called *Great Britain or Industrial Wasteland?* (Polity, 1986, £4.95). The beauty and variety of the country's rivers is captured in *Rivers of Britain* by

Richard and Nina Muir (Michael Joseph, 1986, £14.95), which includes many striking photographs.

There are few places in Scotland where you are far from the sea, and Scotland's inshore waters still provide a considerable number of Scots with their livelihood. But the seas around Scotland are increasingly being used as an all-purpose tip for industrial, domestic and agricultural waste, and at the same time exploitative fishing techniques are in danger of decimating wildlife populations.

North Sea pollution has had a disastrous effect on the Scottish seal population, while overfishing of sand eels around Shetland has led to a massive decline in the breeding populations of several species of seabird. Meanwhile there are still many Scottish beaches, including the favourites at Saltcoats and Irvine on the Clyde coast and North Berwick on the Firth of Forth, which consistently fail the European Community bathing water quality standard.

Greenpeace's beautifully illustrated book, *Coastline* (Kingfisher, 1987, £14.95), chronicles both scenic highlights and environmental threats around the seaboard, while detailed information about the relative cleanliness of Britain's beaches is contained in the Marine Conservation Society's *Good Beach Guide* (Ebury, 1988, £5.95). If you plan to spend some of your holiday swimming and sunbathing, or walking along the coast, you may be very glad of this handy volume to consult.

Natural history and countryside conservation

The rich variety of landscape and habitat in Scotland provides the backdrop to a wide and fascinating variety of plants and animals. Yet because Scotland is a small country, and because some of the people who live in it still feel that they have a right to destroy wildlife and its habitats indiscriminately, there has been an alarming decline in the country's wildlife resources in recent years.

The threat to wildlife sometimes comes from those who are the most well-meaning. The very species that naturalists and the interested public travel many miles to visit can become the victims of their own popularised rarity, and protected sites are often so small that any change in the surrounding area can have tragic results.

The most important advice to any green traveller where wildlife is concerned is to make your presence in fragile habitats as light and as short as possible. The ecological web is a complex one, of which you are a part just as much as the rest of the natural history of the place you are in.

Many visitors to nature reserves and other relatively wild areas know instinctively that the wild inhabitants of those places should be respected; others want to know about those inhabitants and their complex interactions in more detail. Ecological understanding is the key to such wisdom, and there are today literally thousands of amateur naturalists patiently observing and recording their local wildlife, building up a detailed picture of Scotland's fascinating non-human population.

There is a long history of countryside conservation in Scotland, yet at a time when public concern about conservation has never been greater public spending on the countryside is being cut back, to the inevitable detriment of the country's protected areas.

For complex historical and political reasons, Scotland has no national parks, though following the publication of an important Countryside Commission for Scotland report in 1978 called *Scotland's Scenic Heritage*, it was proposed that forty or so 'national scenic areas' should be established, covering about 12% of the country's area. This has now been done, the largest such areas being in the Western Highlands, though other important areas throughout the country have been designated.

At the other end of the conservation scale are Scotland's hundred or so nature reserves, the majority of which are managed by the Scottish Wildlife Trust. Most of these are also owned by the Trust and so have a guaranteed future, though small reserves are often threatened by changes taking place beyond their boundaries; because conservation is the primary aim, public access often has to be strictly limited.

The Scottish Wildlife Trust has its central office in Edinburgh (25 Johnston Terrace, EH1 2NH), with local branches throughout Scotland. The SWT manages more than eighty nature reserves throughout Scotland, provides educational and research facilities, and will be able to put you in touch with a local group if you are spending some time in an area and would like to meet other amateur naturalists. It also publishes an excellent monthly magazine called *Scottish Wildlife*.

The Natural History Book Service (2 Wills Road, Totnes, Devon TQ9 5XN) can supply virtually any book about natural history which is in print, including a wide range of titles of Scottish interest. On receipt of a large stamped addressed envelope they will be happy to send you a copy of their current catalogue.

The Macmillan Guide to Britain's Nature Reserves (1989, £24.95) is a beautifully illustrated and detailed guide to 2,000 reserves all around Britain — a thick volume to be consulted in a library rather than carried around with you.

The Countryside Commission for Scotland (Battleby, Redgorton, Perth PH1 3EW) is an excellent source for material about countryside conservation in Scotland, and much of their literature is free, including their informative newsletter *Scotland's Countryside*. One very useful publication which they have produced in conjunction with the Countryside Commission in England is a map called *Protected Areas in the United Kingdom*. If you slip this into your pocket you can be sure not to miss any important wildlife highlights.

Other organisations concerned with nature and countryside conservation in Scotland include the Association for the Protection of Rural Scotland (14a Napier Road, Edinburgh EH10 5AY), the Scottish equivalent of the influential Council for the Protection of Rural England; the Scottish Wild Land Group (1/3 Kilgraston Court, Edinburgh EH9 2ES), dedicated to conserving and educating people about Scotland's wilderness areas; and the Scottish Scenic Trust (15 Drummond Place, Edinburgh EH3 6PJ), working to achieve better protection for the country's scenic beauty.

Trees and woodland

From the remnants of the original Caledonian pine forest to the open beechwoods of the south of the country, Scotland's trees add immeasurably to the beauty and variety of its landscape. Yet Scotland has retained less of its native woodland than any country in Europe except for England.

Today's forests are very different from Scotland's original tree cover, and many parts of the country have suffered from the indiscriminate planting of immense stands of single-species conifers. Recently, however, the Forestry Commission has begun to recognise that the discriminating traveller appreciates well-planned forestry, and that tourism can be encouraged by the provision of walks through varied forest habitats, information services and volunteer conservation projects.

The Forestry Commission (231 Corstorphine Road, Edinburgh EH12 7AT) produces some excellent material, including two booklets about all the commonest tree species you will find in Scotland: *Conifers* and *Broadleaves* (they cost 25p each). The Ordnance Survey and publishers Webb and Bower have produced a guide to *Woodland Walks in Scotland* (1986, £5.95), including detailed maps and ecological information. The Woodland Trust (54 Manor Place, Edinburgh EH3 7EH) owns and manages woodlands throughout the country, and part of their policy is to encourage public access; they can provide a list of woodlands in their care.

Wildflowers

From the high-altitude alpine delicacy of saxifrage, lady's mantle and moss campion to the bluebell woods of Galloway and the Borders, a wide variety of wildflowers can be found in Scotland. Some, like the beautiful purple *Primula scottica*, are only to be found in this country.

Like so much of our wildlife, however, much of Scotland's flora is under threat. Agricultural practices militate against the proliferation of wildflowers, while some people inexplicably continue to pick rare flowers, even to take whole plants, ignoring that plant's right to survive even though it can't run away and hide.

Alastair Fitter's *New Generation Guide to Wild Flowers* (Collins, 1987, £6.95) is the best of the portable guides, though the Reader's Digest hardback *Field Guide to the Wild Flowers of Britain* (1983, £8.95) is hard to beat for design and user-friendliness. A beautifully written and hauntingly illustrated introduction to the flora of the British Isles is provided by Richard Mabey and Tony Evans in *The Flowering of Britain* (Chatto and Windus, 1989, £10.95). Information about endangered species, together with an illustrated leaflet about protected species, can be obtained from the Fauna and Flora Preservation Society, Regents Park, London NW1 4RY.

Birds

Birdwatching attracts more interest from wildlife amateurs in Scotland than any other subject, which is not surprising when you consider just how rich Scotland is in bird life. Its favoured position at a crossroad of migration routes, together with a rich variety of breeding habitats, provides a rich bounty of birdwatching potential.

Scotland is justly famed for its seabirds: the islands of the north and west are home to some of the largest breeding populations in Europe of species like gannet, guillemot, fulmar and puffin. The mountains support golden eagles, hawks, and the strange-looking capercailzie, while the world-famous observatory on Fair Isle has recorded more than 300 bird species, more than anywhere else in Britain.

Yet at least three dozen bird species have shown an appreciable long-term decline in recent years, including such favourites as the golden eagle and the heron. Pollution, shooting and habitat loss are the main reasons, though birdwatchers must always take care to make their presence as little felt as possible.

The book that any birdwatcher in Scotland should carry is *Where to Watch Birds in Scotland* by Mike Madders and Julia Welstead (Christopher Helm, 1989, £10.95), covering 120 main sites and many additional locations. The best field guide you can buy is *The Shell Guide to the Birds of Britain and Ireland* (Michael Joseph, 1983, £8.95). The Royal Society for the Protection of Birds (17 Regent Terrace, Edinburgh EH7 5BN) is the country's premier ornithological organisation: membership entitles you to free access to their 121 reserves throughout Britain. The Scottish Ornithologists Club (21 Regent Terrace, Edinburgh EH7 5BT) is the organisation for the more serious birdwatcher; their bookshop and mail order service (from the above address) is one of the best bird bookshops in Britain.

The peopled landscape

There are few parts of Scotland where you cannot detect the results of human activity (and a good many places where it is quite hard to discern anything but human activity).

Even the isolated moorlands of the northern highlands and islands remain as they are because they have been grazed and burnt for generations; you only have to explore a small island where this has not happened to see what a difference it makes. It isn't just agricultural activity that has made its mark on what at first sight appears to be open moorland. Many a hill is surmounted by a hillfort, while traces of the platforms of neolithic hillside houses and the lakeside settlements called crannogs can be found in most parts of Scotland, from Shetland to the Galloway hills.

As a result of a century of concern about the built environment, buildings from every period of Scotland's history are now being carefully conserved against the ravages of time and developers. The historical buildings of Scotland are what many visitors come to see (especially on wet days!) and in recent years, as the 'heritage industry' has gathered momentum, many efforts have been made to brighten up the country's buildings, adding exhibitions, displays, tearooms and souvenir shops.

Prehistory

The Scottish landscape is thick with reminders of the country's distant past, and the visitor interested in the early history of Europe will find some of Europe's most impressive monuments here: the stone circles and burial chambers of Orkney, the brochs or tower houses of the West Highlands, and the hillforts of the Scottish borders.

But these are only the highlights, and once you know what you are looking for you will start to discern early field and settlement patterns, neolithic walls running off across the moorland and the lines of ancient roads.

A good general introduction to the prehistory of Scotland, listing many sites as well as giving a general overview, is Richard Feachem's *Guide to Prehistoric Scotland* (Batsford, 1977, £6.95), while Richard Muir's *Countryside Encyclopedia* (Macmillan, 1988, £14.95) provides an introduction to a wide range of particular features, together with suggestions for further reading.

Local museums are a good source of archaeological information, and are usually delighted to answer specific queries. Many ancient monuments in Scotland are looked after by The Historic Buildings and Monuments Directorate (20 Brandon Street, Edinburgh EH3 5RA); membership brings you a useful Handbook and free entrance to all their 330 properties (though remember that entrance to many of the more isolated and less frequented sites is free anyway). The Council for Scottish Archaeology (Royal Museum of Antiquities, York Buildings, 1 Queen Street, Edinburgh EH2 1JD) exists to heighten public awareness of the country's archaeological heritage.

If you are interested in local legend and mystery, you might choose to carry with you either Jennifer Westwood's fascinating and well-researched *Albion: A Guide to Legendary Britain* (Paladin, 1987, £6.95), or Guy Williams' *Guide to the Magical Places of England, Wales and Scotland* (Constable, 1987, £7.95), chock full of headless horsemen, ghostly figures and fiery dragons.

History

Many people like to know something about the history of the places they visit; it helps them to understand why things are how they are, and gives them something of the 'feel' of a place.

To some extent, however, the experience of old things is a physical and emotional one, and it isn't always helped by being told exactly what everything is and exactly what happened in a particular place. Some tourists walk round an abbey or castle, guidebook in hand, hardly looking up to see the very things they have made such an effort to visit.

You can read about the past, but it can also be very instructive to hear at first hand about the past. Thus you can learn a great deal about a place from talking with its older inhabitants, many of whom will be only too delighted to tell you what it was like 'when me mam did the washing in the yard, and when the steam trains were still running.'

This rich heritage of monuments and memories, like the natural heritage of Scotland, is often endangered. It is at risk from those who would either like to get rid of the past altogether in favour of the new, and from those who simply want to sanitise the past and put it in showcases as a money-spinner.

The two best single volume histories of Scotland are T.C. Smout's classic *A History of the Scottish People 1560-1830* (Fontana, 1979, £4.95) and, covering a longer timescale (including recent history), Tom Steel's *Scotland's Story* (Fontana, 1985, £4.95). For the more serious reader who wants detail and copious footnotes, the four-volume *Edinburgh History of Scotland*, published by Oliver and Boyd in 1978, is what you need.

The Historic Buildings and Monuments Directorate (see under 'Prehistory' looks after many important historic buildings in Scotland; another hundred properties are owned and maintained by the National Trust for Scotland (5 Charlotte Square, Edinburgh EH2 4DU). Membership brings you their annual Handbook, full of useful information for visitors, and lets you into almost all of their properties with no further payment.

As with prehistory, museums are a very good source of local information, and nearly every public library has a section of books of local interest which you can consult.

Agriculture and countryside

Many older people in rural Scotland can remember a time when agriculture was a mainstay of the Scottish economy; even forty years ago there were four times as many people working on the land as there are today.

Though Scotland boasts some rich farmland in the fertile lowland river valleys, much of Scotland's farmland is marginal, and a farmer's livelihood depends upon ingenuity and flexibility. This does not fit well with today's mainstream agriculture, where machinery and chemicals are used to achieve enormous yields from large units. Such a system ruthlessly exploits the best land, while many small and part-time farmers face hardship and bankruptcy.

Though still attractive and appealing to the visitor, the heart has gone out of much of rural Scotland. Nearly a quarter of the houses in parts of Galloway are now second homes, while many villages have lost their shop, their school and their 'local'. Because there is little work and no housing they can afford, young people are leaving. Agricultural workers are poorly paid and poorly housed. The main income in many parts of rural Scotland now comes from tourism.

Some areas have managed to develop new employment and livelihood, but it is often precarious and depends on the whims of central government funding. What is needed is more imaginative and sustainable development, otherwise rural Scotland will lose to second-home owners and undiscriminating tourism what little life it still has.

If you want to find out more about traditional rural life in Scotland, a very readable book is Alexander Fenton's *Country Life in Scotland* (John Donald, 1987, £7.50). David Kerr Cameron's *Cornkister Days* (Penguin, 1986, £4.95) is an evocative account of life earlier this century in North-East Scotland.

The Farming and Wildlife Trust (Garvald Grange, Haddington, East Lothian EH41 4LL) helps to co-ordinate farming and wildlife interests in Scotland, while Rural Forum (The Gateway, North Methven Street, Perth PH1 5FP) works with a range of voluntary organisations to improve the quality and condition of rural life in Scotland.

The built environment

The buildings of Scotland show clearly the influence of several different but all very obviously Scottish traditions. The traditional low small-windowed peasant dwelling, turf-roofed in the north and thatched in the south, can still be seen throughout the country, while the later slated and dormered version is similarly ubiquitous. The sixteenth and seventeenth centuries saw the first 'laird's houses' being built, substantial stone houses in their own grounds; while the same period saw the expansion of the cities, both into spacious Georgian squares and terraces but also into seemingly endless streets of gaunt tenements.

Most Scottish towns display a certain amount of Victorian 'Scots Baronial' — civic buildings with turrets and mock fortifications — which help to create the rather severe and four-square look of many urban centres. Though fairly conventional in most matters architectural, there have been some brave and successful experiments in urban design: two of the most ingenious are Edinburgh's Ramsay Gardens, a picturesque cluster of tenements built at the upper end of the Royal Mile by the nineteenth century planning genius Patrick Geddes, and the wonderful Templeton carpet factory alongside Glasgow Green, built in the style of an Italian palace and now used as a small business centre.

No student of architecture will visit Glasgow without visiting the Charles Rennie Mackintosh masterpieces like the Glasgow School of Art, while the Kibble Palace, a fine domed greenhouse in Glasgow's Botanical Gardens, was an engineering marvel in its time.

Most Scots are proud of their built heritage, and though there are still important buildings under threat of demolition, particularly smaller domestic buildings, there is a growing awareness of the importance of preserving what is left while the option still remains.

If you enjoy wandering round cities looking at the buildings, Lewis Braithwaite's *Exploring British Cities* (Black, 1986, £9.95) is a detailed guide, illustrated with fascinating extracts from Victorian Ordnance Survey maps. *The Buildings of Scotland*, the companion series to Nikolaus Pevsner's pioneering *The Buildings of England*, so far only covers Edinburgh, the Lothians, and Fife.

The National Trust for Scotland (see under 'History') maintains many historic buildings, from stately homes to farm buildings, while The Historic Buildings and Monuments Directorate (see under 'Prehistory') looks after a number of older buildings. If the built environment is of particular interest to you, the Scottish Civic Trust (24 George Square, Glasgow G2 1EF) is the country's foremost urban conservation organisation, and will be glad to answer specific enquiries.

The growth of the Greens

Unheard of until recently in its present context, the word 'green' is already in danger of being debased. As one commentator has put it, 'it tends to mean anything even vaguely good and pleasant, and we shall soon all be saying "Have a green day!" ' But 'green', in relation to politics and lifestyle, is an important concept now beginning to come into its own. More and more people are recognising the importance of nature and its processes and cycles, and of the way in which human activities have thrown those systems out of balance. At the same time it is becoming more obvious that human ill-health and dissatisfaction is intimately linked with the destruction of ecosystems and habitats. As we approach the last decade of the twentieth century, it is clear that a radical change is needed in our social and economic systems, and that if we want there to be a future at all, that future must be green.

The main strands of green theory and practice are easy to enumerate, harder to put into practice: using all resources more carefully and thoughtfully; respecting all living things; and being aware that everything that happens in the world is connected. Though this is just a start, it is a useful and commonsense start.

Many groups of people have seen part of this vision over the decades, and to an extent the strength of the green movement arises from the various strands of social and environmental concern explored by those groups. From the environmental angle come the conservationists and wildlife activists. Then there are those whose primary concern has been justice for the Third World, peace and disarmament, women's rights, animal rights, community action, radical health and education, appropriate technology and co-operative working. The last ten years has seen a coming together of these various strands, and the combined forces of the green movement in Scotland are gaining momentum with every passing month.

Green growth in Scotland

Scots seem always to have been fighting for their own rights and those of the land of their birth, and insofar as many of the traditional links with the land are nearer the surface in Scotland than in more urban parts of the western world, most Scots care deeply about their environment.

The recent interest in green concerns dates from the early 1960s, when the pioneering books of Rachel Carson and Paul Ehrlich, John Barr and Max Nicholson alerted their readers to an impending environmental crisis. Women's rights became an important issue, and Scotland's earliest intentional communities (in recent times at least) were founded, such as the Findhorn Foundation in 1967.

To a large extent, many initiatives that would now be thought of as greenish-red were then seen as bright blood red, as communities fought for the right to look after their own affairs, especially in the areas of work and housing. The co-operative movement and community housing initiatives were much needed in urban Scotland, and Strathclyde still leads the way in such community projects. Rural areas too saw some radical experiments in community action, such as the community co-operatives of the Western Isles.

While *Blueprint for Survival*, an early 'green manifesto' produced by the nascent Green Party, was avidly being read by those concerned for the planet's future, Scotland's future was the subject of an important survey published in 1975 called *The Red Paper on Scotland*, which dealt in depth with both social and environmental concerns. Friends of the Earth and Greenpeace started to become influential during the 1970s, the latter being involved in the halting of the Orkney seal cull in the summer of 1978.

Interest in and concern about green issues has never been stronger than it is today. Friends of the Earth Scotland can now run as an autonomous organisation, and the Green Party in Scotland, in line with its policy on Scottish devolution, recently voted to become a separate but linked grouping within the UK Party. If the major conservation organisations like the Scottish

National Trust and the Royal Society for the Protection of Birds are included, it has been estimated that one in twenty Scots are actively involved in environmental groups, while public opinion is firmly behind green policies.

Though a great deal has been achieved in the greening of this beautiful country, much remains to be done and much is still threatened. *The Green Guide to Scotland* will help you to seek out those people and places where the process of environmental (using the word in its widest sense) rehabilitation and protection is under way, and to find those projects designed to sustain the variety and quality of life in this small and vulnerable country.

The growth of the green movement is explored in Jonathon Porritt and David Winner's *The Coming of the Greens* (Fontana, 1988, £3.95), and you will find a detailed account of the growth of the Green Party in Sara Parkin's *Green Parties* (Heretic, 1988, £6.95). For a thorough overview of all things green in Britain today, including many Scottish projects, look into my *Green Pages* (Optima, 1988, £9.99 — a *New Green Pages* is due in April 1990).

For keeping up to date with green concerns, the monthly magazine *Environment Now* is very good, while *The Scotsman on Sunday* has a regular environment column. *Green Scotland* is an irregular publication which may or may not survive until publication of this guide, but the environmental database called IDEAS (Information Database for Environmental Action in Scotland), based at the Environment Centre in Edinburgh (Drummond High School, Cochrane Terrace EH7 4QP), is reliable and up to date.

The Scottish Green Party, which has branches throughout the country, has its headquarters at 11, Forth Street, Edinburgh EH1 3LE, where you can purchase copies of the excellent magazine *Econews*. Friends of the Earth Scotland is at 15 Windsor Street, Edinburgh EH1 5LA; they have a range of publications and can provide information on many environmental topics.

Environmental conservation

Nearly 900,000 Scots belong to one or other of the country's many nature and conservation groups. Although bodies like the Scottish National Trust have been in existence for many decades, the rapid growth of membership of these organisations has been in the last ten years or so. Whether or not all these people follow up their environmental concern with practical action, nobody could say that the Scots are not interested in conserving their natural heritage.

Of the many books covering different aspects of conservation, two that will be of particular use to the green traveller in Scotland are Angela King and Sue Clifford's *Holding Your Ground: An Action Guide to Local Conservation* (Temple Smith, 1987, £5.95), and the *Directory for the Environment*, listing more than 1,400 environmental groups and organisations throughout Britain: the third edition, edited by Monica Frisch, is to be published in 1990 by Green Print. The Countryside Commission for Scotland (Battleby, Redgorton, Perth PH1 3EW) has published a useful free directory of Scottish organisations called *Who's Who In The Environment: Scotland*. *SCENES*, which stands for Scottish Environmental News (Inch Cam, Roseisle, by Elgin), is a useful monthly digest of news items about the Scottish environment.

Wholefoods and the organic movement

Though it has taken Scotland longer than the rest of Britain to wake up to the wholefood revolution, both wholefood distribution and retailing and organic growing are now spreading rapidly. There are wholefood shops in most larger towns and cities, and even supermarket chains are waking up to the inescapable fact that pesticides, additives and complex food processing do not make for healthier food.

Working Weekends on Organic Farms (Pillars of Hercules, Falkland, Cupar, Fife KY7 7AD) organises visits to organic projects, and has also produced a very useful *Directory of Organizations and Training in the UK Organic Movement* (£1), full of annotated entries with addresses and phone numbers of groups and projects. The Soil Association (86-88 Colston Street, Bristol BS1 5BB) has regional lists of organic farms and smallholdings throughout Britain, including Scotland.

The peace movement

Partly as a reaction to the massive military presence on Scottish soil, the peace movement has been very active. In recent years many peace activists have expanded their concerns into a wide spectrum of green issues, which might make it seem that peace is no longer quite such a central issue. Yet the Campaign for

Nuclear Disarmament is still active in Scotland, helping to keep the disarmament ball rolling at a time of thawing global tension.

The best way to keep in touch with the peace movement in Scotland is to subscribe to *Peace News* (8 Elm Avenue, Nottingham NG3 4GF), which carries nationwide listings of groups, actions and events. Scottish CND is at 420 Sauchiehall Street, Glasgow G2 3JD. Malcolm Spaven's book *Fortress Scotland: A Guide to the Military Presence* (Pluto, 1983, £3.95) is a frightening exposé of the country's more than 200 military installations.

The women's movement

The modern women's movement is generally considered to have been born in North America in the mid-1960s; the first Scottish women's groups were established around 1970. A landmark in chronicling the role and status of women in Scotland was the publication of Eveline Hunter's *Scottish Women's Place* in 1978, a survey which was both practical and searching.

The women's movement has achieved a great deal in twenty years, including specific improvements in the standing of women and also in attitudes towards questions of practical sexual politics. Yet in many ways little has changed, and at a time of economic and social pressure women are often in danger of losing any gains that have been made.

The women's movement has always been decentralised, especially in Scotland, and since the Womanzone bookshop in Edinburgh closed down three years ago it has not been easy for women to find out what is going on in Scotland. There is, however, a women's centre in Edinburgh (97 and 101 Morrison Street, Edinburgh EH3 8BX); and Stramullion women's publishing co-operative have produced a very useful reference book: Eveline Hunter's *The Scottish Women's Handbook* (1987, £8.50).

The men's movement

Paralleling the women's movement, though on a much smaller scale, Scotland also has an active men's movement.

The most active section of the Scottish men's movement is the Scotland West Men's Group (27 Queen Mary Avenue, Crosshill, Glasgow G42), who will probably be able to tell you about activities in other parts of the country.

Radical health and education

Many strands make up this section of the green movement, from holistic health practitioners and radical therapy groups to de-schoolers and freeschoolers. Many forms of alternative healing and education are in fact revivals of traditional skills and relationships, having in common the belief that the carer or teacher is in an equal relationship with the client or pupil, and that the process should essentially be 'client-centred', rather than the emphasis being on what the professional thinks the client most needs.

The Institute for Complementary Medicine is the foremost national networking organisation for holistic healing techniques, while the Scottish 'wing' of the British Holistic Medical Association, Whole Person Care (78 Polwarth Terrace, Edinburgh EH11 1NJ) can put you in touch with local groups and practitioners in Scotland.

In education it is more difficult to suggest a single source of information, but the magazine *Green Teacher* (Llys Awel, 22 Heol Pentrerhedyn, Machynlleth, Powys SY20 8DN, Wales) contains up-to-date information about projects and forthcoming events. Scotland's longest-established 'free school' at Kilquhanity near Castle Douglas in south-west Scotland may be visited if an arrangement is made in advance.

The Glasgow-based *Connections* magazine and the Edinburgh-based *4D* magazine (available from wholefood and alternative bookshops) both contain details of practitioners and courses.

Appropriate technology

Tools and techniques which are entirely appropriate to the task in hand have been used by traditional societies throughout the ages. It is because the complex technologies now widespread in the Western world are in many cases so inappropriate that it needed Fritz Schumacher to remind us in the early 1970s that 'small is beautiful'. Since then the concept of appropriate technology has been refined and put to work in many different settings, from bicycles to light rail, preventive medicine to wind power.

A good place for AT enthusiasts to make contact with in Scotland is SCRAM (11 Forth Street, Edinburgh EH1 3LE), which although it stands for 'Scottish Campaign to Resist the Nuclear Menace' is actually a campaigning organisation covering many aspects of AT, though predominantly in energy studies.

Community action

Until very recently it has not been the habit of central and local government in Scotland to ask the inhabitants of a particular area what they really needed in the way of housing and services: 'Be grateful for what you get' was the more usual response.

Things are changing very rapidly, however, as people and communities recognise that they do have the power and can learn the necessary skills to participate in the creation of their own environment. Once one task has been completed successfully, moreover, it shows how much else is possible. Assisted by professional and technical advisers, community-led schemes not only provide people with what they really want; they usually provide employment, save money, and lead to a real sense of co-operation and fulfilment.

The best place to find out about community initiatives in Britain is the bi-monthly *Community Network*, the joint newsletter of the Association of Community Technical Aid Centres, the Town and Country Planning Association and the Royal Institute of British Architects; write for details to ACTAC, Royal Institution, Colquitt Street, Liverpool L1 4DE. ACTAC have recently established a Scottish branch at 58 Fox Street, Glasgow, which is in the process of putting together a database of Scottish community aid projects. The Community Technical Aid Centre (11 Bloom Street, Manchester M1 3HS) has produced a useful series of information sheets about community projects throughout Britain. The Scottish Co-operatives Development Committee, which co-ordinates worker co-operative projects throughout Scotland, is at Templeton Business Centre, Bridgeton, Glasgow G40 1DA.

Practical advice

Where to stay

There are several choices you can make as far as accommodation during your travels is concerned. One of the pleasantest (and cheapest) ways of seeing Scotland is to stay with friends and relations, and since many Scots have families far-flung throughout the world you probably won't find it hard to find a Scottish connection somewhere. Staying with relations for the holidays is a traditional Scottish way of remaking contact and keeping costs down and, though you may find it more difficult to get to know them well, you will usually find Scottish people very hospitable.

An excellent way of making friends and finding interesting places to stay is through an organisation called Servas (the British contact address is 77 Elm Park Mansions, Park Walk, London SW10 0AP). Members of Servas offer free accommodation to each other in exchange for joining in with whatever activities (usually household or community work) the host is involved with. The time limit for a visit is usually two days, and the scheme is only available to registered Servas members.

The next cheapest form of accommodation, though you will need to balance cost against comfort, is camping. Rural Scotland is one of the few places in Britain, indeed in Europe, where you can usually find a suitable site to pitch your tent other than at a recognised campsite, though if you know who owns the land or there is a house anywhere nearby it is polite to ask first. Otherwise there are more than 400 registered camping and caravan sites in Scotland, many of them providing laundry, shower and shopping facilities. Wherever you camp, especially if it is away from a camp site, take sensible precautions about looking after your belongings, leave no traces after you, and respect both the human and wild inhabitants of your chosen site.

Any tourist information office will provide details of campsites in its area, though the Scottish Tourist Board produces *Scotland: Camping and Caravans Park* guide (the 1990 edition costs £2.95), useful if you plan to spend a lot of time on registered campsites. The Great Outdoors magazine includes plenty of advertisements for camping gear as well as articles and news about outdoor activities in Britain.

Some of the earliest youth hostels were established in Scotland, and there are now over 80 hostels offering low-cost self-catering accommodation. Scottish youth hostels range from castles (Carbisdale Castle in Sutherland) to forest bothies, but all offer dormitories, washrooms, a common room and a kitchen. Some also offer family accommodation. Youth hostels can get very busy during school holidays, so book ahead whenever possible during July and August.

The Scottish Youth Hostels Association (SYHA) Handbook can be obtained from the SYHA, 7 Glebe Crescent, Stirling FK8 2JA. You must first be a member of the Association to use the hostels, but you can join at the first hostel you stay at. Members of affiliated organisations in other countries are welcome to use SYHA hostels without further membership payment.

North America has its motels, France its auberges; Scotland has B&Bs — bed and breakfast establishments. Wherever you are in Scotland you will not be far from a B&B, and they are not expensive either, especially in rural areas. In many parts of the country you will still find a comfortable bed and a hearty breakfast for £7 or £8, though in Edinburgh they start at £10 or £12. The majority of B&Bs will also provide an evening meal and a packed lunch, given sufficient notice.

All tourist information centres have an up-to-date accommodation register, and will usually be able to tell you which B&Bs are likely to have rooms free. Most centres will actually book the room for you at no extra charge. Larger information offices are linked into the 'book a bed ahead' (BABA) system, whereby they can find you suitable accommodation almost anywhere in the country; this may involve a small fee.

Hotels also offer bed and breakfast, and of course other meals as well. The small guest-house type hotel can sometimes be as cheap as B&B in a private house (around £10 a night; remember that in Scotland, as in the rest of Britain, hotels charge per person, not per room); pukka hotels, on the other hand, start at around £25 a night, and the extra comfort and service you receive rarely compensates for the price you pay — unless, of course, money is no object! Many hotels now offer cheaper 'mini-breaks' where, especially out of season, two or three day stays cost little more than a single night, especially if you share a room, and children may often stay free.

The authoritative guides to B&Bs and hotels and guesthouses in Scotland are those produced by the Scottish Tourist Board. The 1990 edition of *Scotland: Bed and Breakfast*, with nearly 2,500 establishments to choose from, costs £2.95. *Scotland: Hotels and Guesthouses* costs £4.50. Scottish Farmhouse Holidays (Drumtenant, Ladybank, Fife KY7 7UG) specialises in B&B holidays, usually by the week, on working farms in Scotland.

Several organisations provide lists of accommodation providing for special needs, such as vegetarian or vegan food, non-smoking rooms or cycle storage. These include:

The International Vegetarian Travel Guide, published annually by The Vegetarian Society (Parkdale, Dunham Road, Altrincham, Cheshire WA14 4QG); the 1989-90 edition costs £3.99. The March issue of *The Vegetarian* magazine carries a holiday guide, while a more detailed *Vegetarian Holiday and Restaurant Guide*, compiled by Pauline Davies, is published by Green Print at £2.99. You may still find copies in Edinburgh bookshops of *Vegetarian Edinburgh*, published in 1985, while vegetarian B&Bs in the Highlands are comprehensively listed in *The Vegetarian Guide to the Scottish Highlands* (90p from local bookshops).

The Vegan Holiday and Restaurant Guide is published periodically by The Vegan Society (33-35 George Street, Oxford OX1 2AY); the 1988 edition costs £2.50.

The Cyclists' Touring Club (69 Meadrow, Godalming, Surrey GU7 3HS) produces a members' *Handbook* every two years, which includes lists of bed and breakfast establishments which particularly welcome cyclists.

The Ramblers' Association (12 Mosspark Road, Milngavie, Glasgow G62 8NJ) also has a handbook, *The Ramblers' Yearbook*. This annual publication, available only to members, lists over 2,300 selected B&Bs throughout Britain, including many in Scotland, and makes membership of the association well worth while for this alone.

My favourite 'green accommodation guide', which includes a number of Scottish B&Bs and guesthouses, is Catherine Mooney's *The Complete Healthy Holiday Guide* (Headway, 1989, £6.95); each establishment included in the guide has been especially chosen for its friendly service and attention to detail. All provide a wholefood menu; most are exclusively vegetarian.

Self-catering accommodation is very much on the increase in Scotland, from caravan parks to stately homes which you can rent by the week. This can be quite a cost-effective way of spending a holiday, especially if there are several people in your group and you want to base yourselves in one place.

Activity holidays of all kinds are also becoming increasingly popular. This can be an excellent way of meeting like-minded people, making new friends, and learning new skills. These days you can find an activity holiday covering almost any interest, from rock climbing and skiing to spinning wool and playing the bagpipes. There are also several communities in Scotland offering a full workshop programme: the best-known are the Findhorn Foundation near Inverness and Laurieston Hall in Galloway.

The Scottish Tourist Board's publication *Scotland: Self-Catering* (£4.50 for the 1990 edition) lists nearly 2,000 cottages, houses, flats and chalets which can be rented by the week. Agencies which have a number of self-catering cottages and chalets on their books include the Forestry Commission (231 Corstorphine Road, Edinburgh EH12 7AT); Finlayson Hughes (Bank House, 82 Atholl Road, Pitlochry, Perthshire PH16 5BL — cottages in the Central Highlands); The National Trust for Scotland (5 Charlotte Square, Edinburgh EH2 4DU); Scottish Country Cottages (2d Churchill Way, Bishopbriggs, Glasgow G64 2RW); and G.M. Thompson and Co. (27 King Street, Castle Douglas, Kirkcudbrightshire DG7 1AB — cottages in Galloway).

For activity holidays, the best guide is the Scottish Tourist Board's *Adventure and Special Interest Holidays in Scotland*, a free publication. The STB also produces a leaflet about horse riding and trekking holidays, and two excellent guides called *Hillwalking in Scotland* (£2.25) and *Walks and Trails in Scotland* (£2.50).

If it is more of a peaceful retreat you are looking for, Geoffrey Gerard's *Away From It All* (Lutterworth, £4.95) lists over a hundred spiritual centres and retreat houses throughout Britain, more than a dozen of them in Scotland.

Several of the intentional communities listed in the directory section of the guide offer accommodation, and some a workshop programme. A full list of communities in Britain can be found in the Communes Network book *Diggers and Dreamers* (£4.95), available from bookshops or writing (enclosing an sae) to the Communes Network, Lifespan, Dunford Bridge, Sheffield S30 6TG. The addresses of the communities mentioned above are The Findhorn Foundation, The Park, Findhorn, Forres, Morayshire IV36 0TZ, and Laurieston Hall, Laurieston, Castle Douglas, Kirkcudbrightshire.

Getting around

Where travelling around is concerned, Scotland can seem both a very small and a very large country. Glasgow, Edinburgh, Perth, Stirling and Dundee are a little more than an hour's journey from each other; Aberdeen and Inverness no more than three hours from the capital. Yet once you start making tracks for the further-flung parts, time slows down — especially if you are using public transport. If you leave Glasgow on the 10.15 bus to Uig in Skye, for example, *en route* to the Hebrides, you won't be in Lochmaddy until after eight in the evening. Going to Shetland by boat involves an overnight crossing.

Central Scotland is for the most part densely populated and busy, which means that as you travel you will find yourself in the company of many other travellers, all intent upon getting where they want to go as quickly as possible. Only a couple of dozen miles away, however, on the long single-track roads across the Lammermuirs or the hills of Renfrewshire, you will often have the landscape all to yourself.

In most parts of Scotland, despite cutbacks and threats of more to come, public transport is reasonably adequate, and usually better than most locals (especially those who drive taxis) would have you believe. Yet there are many rural areas which see a bus two or three times a week, and here a car is almost essential. Try not to add to the problems that cars create, however, and use public transport whenever you can during your travels. In the cities a car is simply more trouble than it is worth (just try parking in Edinburgh's New Town on a weekday), quite apart from the environmental damage it causes.

Between the main centres there are very frequent rail and bus services, and in urban areas public transport (if you can find out about it, which often takes some effort) is as efficient as over-crowded roads allow. On the other hand, urban public transport services are neither as reliable nor as well co-ordinated as they could easily be if they were given a much-needed injection of vision and resources.

During the 1960s many of Scotland's railways were closed, including the main lines between Carlisle and Stranraer, and Carlisle and Edinburgh. Now British Rail has started to reopen stations and create new urban lines, and where there is a rail service standards of comfort and efficiency are quite reasonable. Ticket prices (outside the Strathclyde region, where they are subsidised) are relatively expensive compared with buses.

Free train timetables are available for most routes, and the complete British Rail timetable, a bulky volume which also includes services in England and Wales, is good value at £3.50. There are a number of discount schemes available, including a family railcard and a student railcard — both must be bought in Britain when you arrive (for details write to British Rail, PO Box 28, York YO1 1FB). Saver tickets are the cheapest return fares, with an additional discount if you can avoid travelling on Fridays and other peak days. If you are visiting Scotland from abroad and know exactly where you want to go, it is cheaper to buy your rail tickets at the same time as you book your holidays; there are also special schemes like the BritRail Pass, which offers unlimited travel in Britain within a prearranged period of time — these too must be bought before you leave home.

The Railway Development Society has produced an attractive guide called *Scotland by Rail* (£2.75), available from main stations and bookshops.

Nationwide coach services link all the main centres in Scotland, and detailed timetables are available for all routes. Fares are usually around half that of trains, journey times up to twice as long (the fact that it takes nearly twice as much energy to carry a coach passenger as it does a train passenger shows how much hidden support is given to the nation's road system).

Local bus services range from the excellent to the non-existent. Most cities have a good service, especially since mini-buses were introduced in the mid 1980s; it is hard, however, to find out exactly where and when they run, since deregulation in 1988 meant a free-for-all on the roads. Both Glasgow and Edinburgh are planning a more integrated rail/tram/bus transport system, but these are still some years from implementation.

You really do have to be in possession of an up-to-date timetable to be able to use buses in rural areas (or find somebody local who uses them and knows) — bus stops do not generally display information about the routes they serve. It is always worth checking as you board a bus that it is going where you want.

Information about national bus and coach services in Scotland is obtainable from Scottish Citylink at St Andrew Square Bus Station, Edinburgh EH1 3DU, and Buchanan Bus Station, Killermont Street, Glasgow G2 3NP. Scottish Citylink also have a London office at 298 Regent Street, London W1R 6LE, where you can reserve seats and buy tickets for London-Scottish services as well as for services within Scotland.

If you are planning to spend any time in the Highlands and Islands it is well worth buying a copy of *Getting Around the Highlands and Islands*, published biennially by FHG Publications in association with the Highlands and Islands Development Board (the 1990 edition costs £2.50). It contains information about all rail, air, sea and road links, together with useful maps and a resources directory.

It's true that there are plenty of hills in Scotland, but most of the roads go through the valleys, making this excellent cycling country. You can hire bicycles — both touring and mountain bikes — in many places, and there is an active cycling campaign, Spokes, based in Edinburgh (more about them under 'Edinburgh' in the directory). *New Cyclist* quarterly magazine, a fresh new look at the cycling scene, is also based in Scotland.

One thing to be aware of if you are cycling in Scotland is that although you can take your bike on almost any train, the new 'Sprinter' services only have room for two cycles on each train. You can book space to make sure, and there is usually room for everyone who wants to travel with their bike, but in summer the more popular routes can get booked up.

The Cyclists' Touring Club (69 Meadrow, Godalming, Surrey GU7 3HS) is Britain's foremost campaigning group for cyclists; at a hundred years old it likes to think of itself as one of Britain's first 'green' organisations. If you are planning a cycling holiday, it is well worth joining the CTC if only to get their excellent *Handbook* and join their insurance scheme.

Unlike England, Scotland has never had an extensive canal system, and apart from the Caledonian Canal between Inverness and Fort William and the Crinan Canal in Argyll, there are no real working canals left in the country. The Forth and Clyde Canal, built between Edinburgh and Glasgow and opened in 1790, has been blocked in many places by road building and industrial development, but there are still some very pleasant stretches to walk along and sail on.

The British Waterways Board (Canal House, Applecross Street, Glasgow G4 9SP) is the first port of call for anyone interested in Scotland's canals. They produce a wide range of literature, including details of canal boat holidays on the Caledonian Canal.

Whatever other forms of travel you use during your holiday in Scotland, walking is still the most efficient and pollution-free method of travelling short distances, and walking in Scotland will get you to all sorts of wonderful places which other forms of locomotion can never reach. Scotland now has several long-distance paths, pride of place going to the West Highland Way and the Southern Upland Way, and dozens of nature trails, woodland walks and urban heritage trails.

The Scottish Tourist Board publishes two excellent booklets called *Walks and Trails in Scotland* (£2.50) and *Hillwalking in Scotland* (£2.25); the former includes nearly 200 walks from canal towpaths and Edinburgh town trails to long distance footpaths.

The Ramblers Association (12 Mosspark Road, Milngavie, Glasgow G62 8NJ) provides a wide range of services to walkers, including their invaluable *Ramblers' Yearbook* and access to their comprehensive map library.

Compared with most of Europe, hitchhiking in Scotland is relatively easy, at least outside the built-up areas of Central Scotland. Indeed, a lot of young locals do it, since it is often the only way to get where they want to quickly enough. Be warned that in summer a lot of traffic in rural areas consists of families on holiday with a car full of luggage; hitchable vehicles are few and far between.

Most advice to do with thumbing lifts is common sense: look after yourself, refuse any lift you don't like the look of, stand in a safe place where vehicles can stop easily, look as though you want to go somewhere and will be good company for the duration, and don't be too concerned about exactly where you end up.

There are several books about hitch-hiking in Britain, like Ken Lussey's *Hitch-Hikers' Guide to Great Britain*, but if you know anything at all about thumbing lifts you won't need a book. Just make sure that you have a good map, good waterproofs, and that you don't stand where everyone else is standing.

What and where to eat

Scots like both their food and their drink, but many Scots are not very discriminating about either, which goes a long way towards explaining why Scotland has the highest rates of heart disease, tooth decay and liver failure in the world. Fish and chip shops (remember to ask for 'a fish supper' rather than 'fish and chips' if you want to sound like a native) abound, as do off licences, Chinese takeaways and Italian ice cream and sweetie shops.

Healthy eating has come late to the country, and is still to a large extent the preserve of the incomer ruralites and the yuppie urbanites. While you will find a reasonably balanced menu in up-market city centre restaurants and a few enlightened rural eating places, the middle ground of microwaved readi-meals can be pretty dire.

Cooked breakfast, often with black pudding accompanying the bacon and eggs, is the rule rather than the exception at B&B establishments, the vegetarian alternative being packet cereal and diluted fruit juice.

Lunchtime is usually around 1pm, and in smaller towns many shops still close between 12.30 and 1.30 or 1 till 2. Traditionally the midday meal was the main meal of the day, with a 'high tea' (mostly farinaceous but usually with a hot course) following after work at about 5.30 and a light snack at bedtime. An increasing number of people, however, now follow the 'English' pattern of having their main meal in the evening, which usually better serves the traveller.

Many restaurants, especially of the fast food variety, now open throughout the day (except on Sunday, when opening hours are reduced or non-existent). Others will often serve lunch between 12 noon and 2pm (often with a cheaper 'businessperson's lunch' as well as the a la carte menu), then dinner from 7 until 10pm. The cities boast a wide range of restaurants from many different cultures, though the Italian influence is particularly strong. In smaller towns restaurant menus will usually be simpler and more basic, though country house hotels can often provide excellent fare — at a price.

The traditional Scottish beverage is supposedly the dram, and many are undoubtedly downed every night, but the real national drinks are tea and McEwans, neither very good for the Scottish digestion. The real ale movement has reached Scotland, however, and several local brewers produce some good home-brewed beers.

There are several guides to eating out in Scotland, though tourist information offices will give you the most up-to-date information. At the cheaper end of the range of restaurants is the annual *Cheap Eats* (Hodder and Stoughton, £5.95), while if you want Scottish cookery at its very best, the Scottish Tourist Board's *The Taste of Scotland Guide* (annual, £2.20 for the 1990 edition) lists nearly 200 establishments which have been awarded the special 'soup tureen' plaque for excellence.

For vegetarians and vegans, as well as the accommodation and restaurant guides listed on pages 38-39 there is also Sarah Brown's *Best of Vegetarian Britain* (Thorsons, £4.99) which includes a fair number of Scottish restaurants.

The real ale movement in Britain is spearheaded by the Campaign for Real Ale (CAMRA, 34 Alma Road, St Albans AL1 3BW), who publish the annual *Good Beer Guide* (the 1990 edition costs £4.95), which contains full details about breweries and where you can buy their brews.

What to take with you

The answer to this is simple; the application of it often less so: 'As little as you possibly can.' When planning what to carry with you, either for the holiday as a whole or for a day's outing, it is often helpful to ask yourself the ultimate green question: 'But do I really need it?' If you are in doubt, leave it; it's amazing what human beings can do without, especially when they are supposed to be relaxing on holiday!

Around your person, preferably in a zipped pocket, keep money, passport, tickets, your travel plans and timetables for the day. In an easily accessible place have the map, a book for reading during unplanned delays, and your address book and diary. Providing you dress appropriately before you set out, this is probably all you will need for a day's outing.

If you take lightweight cotton clothes, a couple of sweaters and several pairs of warm socks, and wear your heaviest coat or anorak when travelling so it doesn't take up luggage space, your clothing shouldn't take up too much room, especially if you are travelling in summer. A good pair of trainers and a pair of sandals should be sufficient footwear unless you are planning some rough mountain walking; rubber wellington boots can usually be provided by the friends who invite you to wade through the mud with them.

You can often leave at least part of your luggage with friends while you travel, and you can always post some of it home if you know you won't need it again on this trip. All main railway and bus stations have left luggage offices, and some information offices in rural areas will keep an eye on your things for you.

There are now many places where you can hire camping equipment, so unless you have very lightweight equipment or are planning to spend a lot of time under canvas think carefully whether you need to bring your own stuff. Modern camping equipment is very compact and light, as are today's rucksacks. On the other hand, unless you are doing a lot of walking a rucksack can sometimes be more of a nuisance than a soft bag. There is always the temptation to fill a large rucksack just because it's there.

The best maps of Scotland are produced by the Ordnance Survey, whose main office in Scotland is at the Edinburgh Map Centre, 51 York Place, Edinburgh: they will gladly send you a copy of their catalogue. The Routemaster maps cover Scotland in 4 sheets at 1:250,000, and are excellent for travelling by public transport or bicycle. If you are walking in one particular area, you will want the relevant Landranger map; these cover Scotland in 83 sheets at 1:50,000. Even more detailed are the Pathfinder 1:25,000 maps; it takes nearly 550 of these to cover the country, but they do show every wall, house and hillock. Ordnance Survey maps are not cheap, but they are detailed, accurate, and a joy to look at.

Many regions and towns produce very good basic maps of their areas, and you can nearly always get a simple free map of the neighbourhood from tourist information offices.

Clothing, camping equipment and many of the other things you may need on your travels are relatively cheap in Scotland compared with most other northern European countries, and similar to those in the USA, another good reason for not carrying round more than you really need.

Health

Because travelling involves many new experiences and a great deal of effort (however 'restful' you expect it to be), it can at the same time be exhilarating and tiring, stimulating and stressful. It is very important to look after yourself on your travels, giving yourself time to relax and calm down occasionally before embarking on the next outing. Try to eat a sensible healthy diet, and don't be tempted by sweetie shops and fast food establishments. Get some exercise, too; if you're not walking or cycling it can sometimes be difficult to exercise properly when you are travelling.

If, despite looking after yourself, you find yourself not feeling too well, there are several things you can do. Most chemists' shops in Scotland have a pharmacist on hand to suggest an appropriate remedy, and they generally like to be consulted, so don't pretend that you know what you need if you don't. Many chemists' shops these days also carry a range of homeopathic (and perhaps even some herbal) remedies.

There are also a growing number of practitioners of complementary and alternative healing techniques in Scotland. Most umbrella organisations (for acupuncture, herbalism, etc.) have a national referral service, and you can often find practitioners either through *Yellow Pages* or through cards on wholefood shop and alternative bookshop noticeboards.

The British National Health Service, set up in 1946, provides a comprehensive medical service to everyone normally resident in the country; there are also reciprocal arrangements with health services in other countries. If you are not a British citizen and have an accident or are suddenly taken ill, there will usually be no hesitation in providing you with the facilities you need; the emergency services in Scotland are on the whole excellent. On the other hand, the NHS is very drugs-and-surgery oriented, and has been dubbed the National Illness Service by some observers, since along with medical establishments throughout the Western world it still seems to be more interested in symptoms and cures than in health and preventatives.

It is hard to know what to advise where health insurance is concerned; the whole idea of putting cash values on lost lives and limbs is anathema to most green-thinkers, yet if a drunken driver should take aim at you it will be at least a little comfort that the insurance company will get you home without your having to fork out. Think carefully about your priorities and responsibilities before you buy travel insurance, then get some good professional advice.

If you are not British and need the services of the NHS, the bureaucratic details will usually be dealt with automatically; if you are interested in knowing in advance what reciprocal medical arrangements exist between your country and Britain, you can write for a leaflet to DHSS (Leaflets), PO Box 21, Stanmore, Middlesex HA7 1AY.

The Institute for Complementary Medicine (21 Portland Place, London W1N 3AF) runs a telephone referral service on 01-636 9543, and has plans for a comprehensive guide to holistic practitioners in Britain. The ICM also runs a regional 'public information point' service; regional telephone numbers within this service are given later in the guide under specific regions (where such a service exists). Whole Person Care (78 Polwarth Terrace, Edinburgh EH11 1NJ; Tel: 031 337 8474), the Scottish branch of the British Holistic Medical Association, also has lists of practitioners in Scotland, while the Glasgow-based *Connections* magazine contains a detailed list of groups and practitioners in the fields of healing and therapy.

In an emergency, simply dial 999 from the nearest telephone — the call is free — and ask for an ambulance. Speed is often vital, especially if someone has lost consciousness.

Language and dialect

Scotland has two — some would say three — languages. There is English, the language that everybody speaks and understands; then there is the Gaelic, spoken by nearly 80,000 people mostly in the Western Highlands and the Western Isles; and then there is Scots with its heartland in the north-east lowlands, and about which there has always been debate as to its status — is it a dialect or is it a language?

Until a hundred years ago Gaelic was a major Scottish language and there were many thousand for whom it was their only tongue. It still has its strongholds and a thriving cultural infrastructure, including books, newspapers and festivals. Attention is also being focused on the rich vocabulary of the Scots language, and this is helping it too to survive.

The regions of Scotland have retained their distinctive language patterns far better than most parts of England, and it is quite an education to listen to conversations in shops, bars and workplaces. Even if you have never been to Scotland before you will not fail to notice the soft closed vowels of the Hebrides, the harder and more guttural sound of Aberdonian speech, or the Jean Brodie-like twang of Morningside Edinburgh.

Like the English, Scots are not good at learning other people's languages; when abroad they speak English and expect foreigners who visit their country to do the same. You will, however, find a few people who are able to communicate in French, German or Norwegian, and you will also find that Scots are quite patient; if they know you have something important to say, they won't give up easily!

The interests of Gaelic speakers are looked after by the Inverness-based organisation An-Comunn Gaidhealach (109 Church Street). The richness of the Scots tongue can be glimpsed by looking into *The Concise Scots Dictionary*, published by Aberdeen University Press, while Billy Kay's book *Scots: The Mither Tongue* (Mainstream, 1986) argues passionately for maintaining regional differences in Scottish dialects and pronunciations.

Money

Most Scottish people are very trusting where money is concerned. Except at American-style fast food outlets you will not need to pay for a meal until you leave, and B&Bs and hotels will gladly put everything on your bill for you to pay at the end of your stay. If you drop something in the street, the chances are that somebody will notice and give it back to you.

Scotland's currency is identical to that of England, except that the three major Scottish banks issue their own colourful banknotes; though these are legal tender throughout Britain you may have problems the further south you go, especially with Scottish £1 notes now that the Bank of England £1 note has been replaced by a coin.

Remember that many British banks have a strange habit of closing at 3.30 in the afternoon, and some smaller branches also close between 12.30 and 1.30pm. Post offices close at 12.30 on Saturdays. Travellers cheques can be used as currency in a wide range of places, and credit cards — whatever you think of the ethics involved — are useful in restaurants, shops and railway stations.

If you are a resident of the European Community, you can earn money in Scotland quite legitimately, and some long-term travellers finance their travels by taking seasonal work. Residents of other countries should technically have a work permit, though you can always barter your work or skills in exchange for accommodation or travel.

Approaching people and organisations

In general you will find that people are delighted if you show an interest in their pet project; even more delighted if you offer to help. There are a few commonsense considerations, however, which will help you to make the most of the contacts you make during your travels:

— Be discriminating about the contacts you make, and be as clear as possible about what you want. If you are interested in visiting craft co-operatives, for example, it will almost certainly be more productive to write individual letters to three or four, explaining your interest and experience, than to send a standard photocopied letter to every company listed in the Scottish Development Association Crafts Directory.

— Always (unless the organisation you are writing to is a public body or a large commercial business) enclose either a stamped addressed envelope or envelope re-use label, or an international reply coupon. Most green-tinted organisations do not have the resources to support large postage bills.

— If you plan to visit (unless your planned port of call is a recognised tourist attraction), always give advance notice. Writing well ahead is best, though since people are not always very good at replying, it is a good idea to check the arrangement by phone a day or two ahead of your visit.

— Try to be sensitive to the needs of the people and project you are visiting. Many people involved in greenish activities are good and fascinating talkers, especially when they encounter people who are as enthusiastic as they are about their project, but they do tend to lead busy and unpredictable lives. They can turn out to be so involved that they have become green bores, but *you* will have to deal with that problem!

— If you stay for meals or are driven round a project — anything that involves expense on your host's part — do at least check whether payment is in order. Small and appropriate gifts will almost always be appreciated, especially a little cash help with the project.

If you go about things in the right way you will almost always be very welcome to visit green initiatives. But you can't expect to be cossetted in the way that organised coach parties are.

Handicapped travellers

Most of us have experienced the frustrations of crowded trains, closed restaurants and busy city streets; imagine how much harder it is for someone who can't walk, or see, or hear. Yet people with disabilities are barred from the things that able-bodied people take for granted not so much by their disability, as by the way their surroundings take no account of their particular problems. The solution is often very simple: a ramp instead of a step, a door that opens the other way, a dropped kerb at a road crossing. It is only recently that the designers of tourist facilities have seriously started to consider the needs of handicapped people, but now that awareness is growing things are rapidly beginning to change for the better. In drawing the attention of the tourist industry to the needs of handicapped travellers, the Scottish Tourist Board has helped a great deal.

The Scottish Tourist Board works hard to make sure that handicapped people are not denied the access and facilities afforded to the able-bodied. Nearly all of their guides include information about such things as access and special facilities for blind or deaf people, and the STB and the Highlands and Islands Development Board have produced a booklet called *Providing for Disabled Visitors* to help those involved in the tourist industry to understand what is needed. The Scottish Council on Disability (Princes House, 5 Shandwick Place, Edinburgh EH2 4RG) has an information department which can tell you about almost every aspect of equipment, facilities and advice available to the handicapped traveller.

Travelling with children

Travelling with children can be tiring and limiting, but it doesn't have to be. In many ways Scotland is ideally suited to a child's needs: plenty of open space and the freedom to explore it. Children will inevitably change the pace of your travelling: their attention span tends to be relatively short, so museum trips may have to be curtailed, but you may also be asked to spend hours looking at rock pools and spiders webs.

You will almost certainly need to plan more in advance, making bookings on public transport and ensuring that you have somewhere to stay — the 'book a bed ahead' scheme (see page 37) is very useful in this respect. Given foresight, flexibility and patience, travelling with children can be an enjoyable and fulfilling experience for all concerned.

A very useful book to have with you if you are travelling with children is Betty Jerman's *Kids' Britain* (Pan, 1986, £2.95), full of interesting places and ideas about things to see and do. The Scottish Tourist Board publishes an annual booklet called *Scotland: A Land for Young People*, with details of everything from language schools to special interest holidays. Local tourist information offices will usually be able to tell you about events which might particularly interest the younger members of your party.

The Northern Isles

Shetland

Shetland and Orkney became part of Scotland almost by accident, for until the mid-fifteenth century they belonged to Norway. The islands were pledged for 58,000 Rhenish florins to provide the dowry for the Norwegian Princess Margaret on her marriage to James

Orkney

III of Scotland in 1468, but because the royal coffers were temporarily empty the pledge was never redeemed.

The northern islanders, and especially the Shetlanders, are proud and knowledgeable about their history, and the local

dialects and placenames still contain many words of Scandinavian origin. In many ways the northern isles are the most distinctive region of Scotland, and they well repay proper attention — don't try to rush them. A week's restful holiday on one of the smaller islands such as Fair Isle, Foula or Hoy will refresh and inspire you far more than a week's hectic sightseeing.

Shetland is spectacular, with high sea cliffs and narrow inlets, fascinating archaeological sites, and an immense wealth of wildlife, especially seabirds. The islands are really best seen from the sea so, if you have time, take the overnight boat from Aberdeen and wake up early to see Sumburgh Head rising to port. Though Lerwick is charming, with Commercial Street and the narrow lanes winding up the hill, make sure that you get out into the countryside and away from the main roads. Take a ferry to Fetlar, Papa Stour or Bressay (just across the harbour from Lerwick) and then walk with the wind blowing through your hair.

The mountainous southern island of Hoy apart, the islands of Orkney lie low in the water, 'like sleeping whales' is how Orkney writer George Mackay Brown describes them. Like Lerwick, Kirkwall has a very special charm, grouped tightly around the rugged cathedral of St Magnus, while Stromness, Orkney's second town which grew rapidly as a port in the eighteenth century, has a seaside feel to it. Of Orkney's many archaeological sites Maeshowe, Skara Brae and the stone circles at Stenness and Brogar are but the brightest jewels, while many people come to Orkney to see the seals (sadly decimated in recent years by pollution-borne disease) and the seabirds.

Regional Tourist Offices: Shetland Tourist Organisation, Information Centre, Market Cross, Lerwick, Shetland ZE1 0LU (Tel: 0595 3434); Orkney Tourist Board, Information Centre, Broad Street, Kirkwall, Orkney KW15 1DH.

Ancient Sites: The remarkable preservation of the northern isles' ancient monuments is due largely to the abundance of hard flagstone for building and the absence of any other building material. Skara Brae, the neolithic stone village hidden for centuries under the sand, is remarkable for its completeness, as are the wheelhouses at Jarlshof in Shetland which date from the same period. As impressive are the burial chambers from this period, which are between three and five thousand years old: Maeshowe in Orkney, where only the midwinter sun aligns with the entrance passage, is awe-inspiring, so try to avoid peak visitor times. Other burial chambers include the 'stalled cairn' at Midhowe on the Orkney island of Rousay and the Dwarfie Stane on Hoy, a massive block of sandstone into which a chamber has been carved.

On to stone circles, the great monuments at Stenness and Brogar were completed around four thousand years ago, as was the Haltadans circle on Fetlar — the two stones at the centre of this circle are said to be the 'trowie fiddler' and his wife. On another fifteen centuries into the bronze age, and the northern isles have some of the most complete brochs in Britain. These tower houses, probably built for communal protection, can be seen at Gurness and Midhowe in Orkney, though the best is on the small southern Shetland island of Mousa (boat trips are organised from Leebitten on the Mainland).

The Picts found their way to the islands in the iron age, leaving carved symbol stones which can be seen in the museums at Lerwick and Kirkwall, to be followed in historical times by the Vikings.

Trees and Woodland: The northern isles are almost devoid of trees save for small plantations in very sheltered places. Town gardens contain mature sycamores and other trees, often the subject of preservation orders, but elsewhere saplings reach walltop height and then give up the unequal struggle with the wind.

Wildlife: Ever since the first naturalists visited the northern isles two centuries ago they have been acknowledged to contain species of plants and animals unknown elsewhere in Britain, including several known only on one small island. In particular the islands are a birdwatchers' paradise: surrounded by a sea full of fish (or at least until fishermen started gutting the sea of all its marine life, including the sand eels which are many seabirds' staple diet), at the junction of temperate and sub-arctic zones, and at the crossroads of migration routes, Shetland and Orkney welcome thousands of 'twitchers' each year. Fair Isle is the birdwatchers' mecca, boasting an impressive list of rare species as well as large breeding colonies of fulmar, guillemot, kittiwake and puffin. You can see seals in Shetland if you know where to go, but Orkney is even better for them; if you are interested in seals and want to help protect them from the viral disease currently threatening to reduce their numbers substantially, contact Orkney Seal Rescue at Dyke Road, South Ronaldsay. There is also a seal sanctuary at Hillswick in Shetland.

Protected Areas: Almost the entire western coastline of Shetland has been designated a National Scenic Area, as has the Orkney island of Hoy. There are four National Nature Reserves in Shetland: Hermaness and the Keen of Hamar in Unst, Haaf Gruney, and the spectacular cliff-girt island of Noss. The Unst reserves are the most accessible; Noss can be visited in the summer when a warden is in residence.

Access to the Countryside: You can walk almost anywhere in Shetland and Orkney as long as you respect people's gardens, animals and growing crops. Take care as you walk along high clifftops, and in the spring and early summer avoid seabird nesting grounds — arctic terns and skuas will soon let you know that your presence is not welcome.

Organic Initiatives: At Ollaberry in Shetland is an organic smallholding which produces vegetables and some free-range eggs; organic produce can occasionally be purchased at Scoop Wholefoods in Lerwick (Old Infant School, King Harald Street). Breckan Rabbits on the Orkney island of Sanday sells additive-free (though not strictly organic) rabbit meat and paté, both at the farm and by mail order.

Local Building Traditions: Long low crofthouses dominate the rural landscape, while the towns cluster together in an organic higgeldy-piggeldy way. Lerwick's town centre, now a conservation area, is particularly attractive, and the many lanes that run between Commercial Street and the Hillhead offer a pleasant stroll on a summer's evening. Orkney Islands Council Planning Department has produced excellent illustrated *Heritage Guides* to Kirkwall and Stromness.

Museums: As well as the Shetland Museum on the Lower Hillhead (above the library, which houses an excellent collection of local material), other Shetland museums to make a point of visiting are the Böd of Gremista, a restored eighteenth century fishing booth just north of Lerwick, and the Croft House Museum at Boddam, where a thatched cottage and outbuildings have been restored to appear as they might have been in the mid-nineteenth century. In recent years a number of small local museums and interpretative centres have been opened around Shetland, and are well worth a visit.

Kirkwall library has a good collection of material of local interest, while Stromness Natural History Museum also contains historical items. Museums set in restored traditional farmhouses can be visited at Corrigall, Harray, and Kirbister near Birsay.

Communal Groups: In most parts of the islands, community life is still vital in a form that is now rare elsewhere in Britain, with people helping each other in vital tasks like harvesting and peat cutting. The small western Shetland island of Papa Stour probably owes the fact that it is still inhabited to an initiative in the early 1970s to attract young people to the island: some are still there, ensuring a future for the island school and shop.

Community Initiatives: Shetland has a small but active Shetland Environmental Group: contact them through Scoop Wholefoods (see 'Organic Initiatives'). Among other things the Shetland Amenity Trust (22-24 North Road, Lerwick) organises is a regular clean-up of roadside verges, which would otherwise become liberally scattered with multicoloured beer-cans, and it also has an extensive environmental improvement programme.

Co-operatives: Scoop Wholefoods in Lerwick is a co-operative, as is Simply Shetland, a knitwear business in North Roe which provides much-needed employment in this remote area. Other Shetland co-operatives include Fair Isle Knitwear and North Isles Community Enterprise.

Craft Workshops: There is a strong tradition of furniture making in Orkney, especially of the tall cane-backed chairs known as Orkney chairs: you can see them being made in Kirkwall by Robert Towers (Rosegarth, St Ola) and D.M. Kirkness (14 Palace Road), and at Westray Strawback Chair Products on Westray. Maiden Evie at Hopedale House, Birsay is a company making handmade pure cotton clothes.

The Shetland Workshop Gallery in Lerwick displays a wide selection of imaginative local crafts, and at Broadfoot on the remote Shetland island of Foula you can do week-long courses in spinning and weaving.

Anti-Nuclear Initiatives: Only a few miles across the Pentland Firth from the southern coast of Orkney is the nuclear fast breeder reactor at Dounreay, where the British government also has plans to store nuclear waste. CADE, the Campaign Against Nuclear Dumping, has a strong and vocal presence in both Orkney and Shetland: for information contact 22 Commercial Road, Lerwick (Shetland CADE) or Snowberry, East Road, Kirkwall (Orkney CADE).

Alternative Energy: The traditional fuel of the northern isles is peat, dug and dried in the summer and burned during the winter. You can see freshly dug peat banks throughout the islands, and if your holiday is in June or July it shouldn't be too hard to find someone willing to let you try your hand with the tushkar, the specially shaped peat spade.

For many days of the year the wind blows relentlessly over the Northern Isles, making them the perfect location for experiments in wind power. At Burgar Hill, north of Stromness in Orkney, is one of the world's largest wind generators, and there is a smaller one on Susetter Hill near Voe in Shetland. Sometimes the wind can be too strong for such generators, and in the winter of 1988 a large machine near Scalloway in Shetland was blown down. Unfortunately, because of electricity pricing policies and high rateable values on wind generators, there is insufficient financial incentive for such experiments, though the inhabitants of the outlying Shetland islands of Foula and Fair Isle are currently exploring ways of helping to make their communities self-sufficient in energy. As well as wind generators which are already operational, there have also been proposals for using wave energy.

Boardhouse Mill at Birsay in Orkney is the islands' last remaining working water mill, specialising in beremeal (an ancient form of barley) and oatmeal which were once island staples. A small traditional watermill, of which there were once thousands in the islands, has been renovated at the Croft House Museum at Boddam in Shetland, while a similar mill at Quendale is being restored by the Shetland Amenity Trust.

Transport: Public transport in the islands is not particularly good; most services run to and from the centres of Lerwick and Kirkwall. There are connecting services of buses and ferries to the larger outer islands, and most of the ferry services, especially in Shetland, are frequent and efficient. If you are feeling rich, Loganair run an island-hopping service to most of the inhabited islands in both Orkney and Shetland, and this is an impressive if passive way of getting to places like Fair Isle and Foula.

The islands are good places for cycling, and there is no problem taking your bike on the inter-island ferries. Bicycles can be hired in Orkney from Paterson's Cycle Centre in Kirkwall (Tankerness Lane) and in Shetland from Shetland Cycle Hire, 19 Market Street, Lerwick.

Health: Though the National Health Service provides a full range of services in the islands, there is little provision for alternative therapies beyond the occasional visiting osteopath and acupuncturist.

Food: Northern islanders traditionally ate a balanced but unvarying diet based on fish, potatoes and oatmeal. Local seafood is well worth trying, and Orkney has a number of other local specialities, including a fine mature cheese and a sticky, tooth-rotting but creamy hard fudge, known as tablet.

Good wholefood meals are not easy to find in local restaurants, though mention should be made of Trenabies Restaurant in Kirkwall (16 Albert Street) which always has a vegetarian option. If you are looking for wholefoods, Scoop in Lerwick (see under 'Organic Initiatives') is Britain's most northerly wholefood shop.

Bookshops: Orcadians and Shetlanders are traditionally voracious readers, which is reflected in the quality of the island bookshops. Shetland is particularly fortunate in having the well-stocked Shetland Times Bookshop at 75 Commercial Street, Lerwick.

Local Directories: A local green-tinted guide called *The Shetland Directory* is planned for publication in 1990; look out for it.

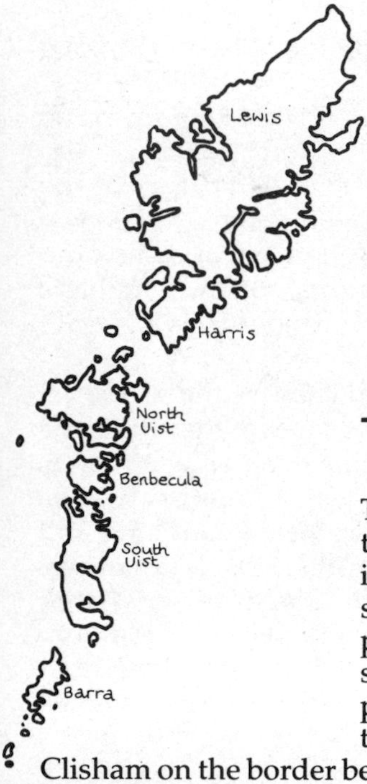

The Outer Hebrides

The map shows the following labels: Lewis, Harris, North Uist, Benbecula, South Uist, Barra.

The Outer Hebrides, or Western Isles as they are called administratively, form an island chain 150 miles from north to south. Here the oldest rocks in Europe push their backbone out of the sea, swelling in rounded moorland in most places, but sometimes rising to mountains more than 2,000 feet high, as at Clisham on the border between Lewis and Harris. The moorland is blanketed with peat and every hollow filled with water, making the land for the most part difficult to till and keeping human settlement to the coastal strip.

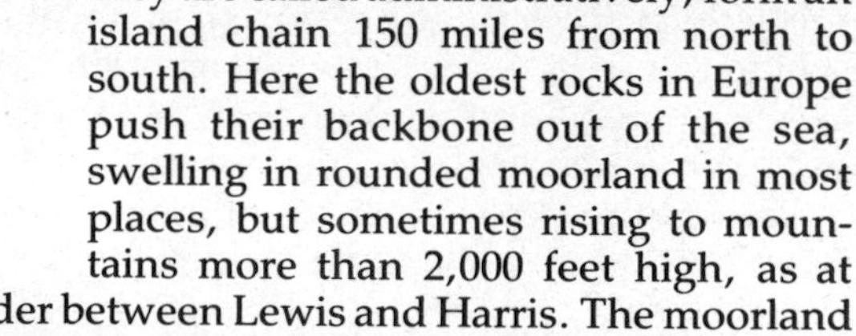

Along the west coast, however, and particularly in the southern islands of North and South Uist, another landscape feature ensures that farming is made possible, for here is a strip of fertile grassland based on the crushed shells of countless numbers of sea creatures washed up on the western edge of the Atlantic. This *machair* land explains why the Uists and Barra have more grazing ground and nearly as much tillage as Lewis

and Harris, even though only one third of the area of the 'long isle'.

Though the land and the sea still provide a living for many people, tourism is a mainstay of the island economy, supplemented by work for the military (South Uist in particular has a major missile-tracking station and artillery range, while even remote St Kilda is dominated by a paraphernalia of dishes and aerials). Still the heartland of Gaelic culture in Scotland, emphasis on the importance of this living tradition is now growing again after half a century of relative stagnation.

Because the Outer Hebrides are dominated by the sea, it is a good idea to travel by boat when you can; as well as the scheduled ferries you can often find someone willing to show you islands and coves which can only be reached by water. Walk or cycle the back roads (the main ones, especially in Lewis, are long and boring): try the road to Hushinish in north Harris, for example, where the beach and the views across to Scarp are wonderful. Leave the road and walk out to Toe Head at Harris's southern extremity (the view from the summit of Chaipival taking in St Kilda and the Skye Cuillins is tremendous), or climb Heaval on Barra for similar exhilaration. And don't miss the standing stones at Callanish.

Regional Tourist Office: Outer Hebrides Tourist Board, 4 South Beach Street, Stornoway, Isle of Lewis PA87 2XY (Tel: 0851 3088).

Ancient Sites: The jewel of the Hebrides' many ancient sights is 'The False Men' or *Fir Chreig*, the impressive stone circle at Callanish on Lewis's west coast. It stands aloof and mysterious on its promontory, and there are many legends associated with the stones: at sunrise on midsummer's day, for example, 'The Shining One' is wont to walk along the adjoining avenue of stones, heralded by the call of the cuckoo, the magic bird of the magic land of the ever-young, *Tir-nan-Og*. Nearby at Dun Carloway is one of the best-preserved iron age broch towers in Scotland, still standing thirty feet tall.

Trees and Woodland: What little native scrub woodland the Outer Hebrides possess can be seen on a few freshwater islets and under sheltered cliffs, but most of the islands' sparse tree cover has been planted in the last century and a half. Shelter belts of conifers have been established around some townships, while the most substantial wood is that surrounding Lews Castle at Stornoway, a mature mixed woodland of native and exotic trees which has attracted a number of birds and animals found nowhere else in the islands, including the Outer Hebrides' only rookery.

Wildlife: Nearly three hundred species of bird have been sighted in the Outer Hebrides: the populations of corncrake, mute swan and greylag goose are of national significance. The outlying islands support large populations of gannet, Leach's petrel and puffin. Grey seals are a common sight; in Stornoway harbour are several which have become quite tame, living on the waste products of the fishing fleet. Otters are also relatively common.

Protected Areas: Three areas of the Western Isles have been designated National Scenic Areas: South Lewis, Harris and North Uist; The South Uist Machair; and St Kilda. St Kilda, a now-uninhabited group of dramatic volcanic islands with sheer cliffs up to 370 metres high teeming with seabirds, is also a World Heritage Site.

Access to the Countryside: There are few places in the region where you cannot walk, though the going can be quite difficult, especially in marshy areas. Jane Twelves, Uist Wildlife Holidays, (Locharnan, South Uist) and Crofting Life Holidays (Bridge House, 20 Bridge Street, Inverness) both offer small group holidays especially for walkers and people interested in getting to know more about the islands.

Organic Initiatives: Keose Co-op on the north side of Loch Erisort in Lewis produces organic fertiliser from dried seaweed.

Museums: Dotted about the islands are small cottage museums. On Lewis, Historic Scotland have preserved a typical crofter's 'black house' at Arnol, while the Shawbost Folk Museum (Shawbost School), also on Lewis, has a display relating to village life.

Community Initiatives: Peat cutting represents a community activity of major importance. Although some commercial cutting takes place, much is still done by hand with groups of neighbours and friends coming together in May to cut the peat which is then left to dry and stacked in piles. From an ecological point of view, peat digging breaks up the hard surface crust, letting in nutrients and water to replenish the acidic soil.

Community projects of various sorts abound, ranging from the Western Isles Care and Repair project set up by Age Concern, to *Proisect Muinntir Nan Eilean*, a community education project focusing on pre-school children and their mothers and led by the parents themselves. 'Women in Barra' and 'Women in Benbecula' discussion groups have recently been established, while other community initiatives have involved groups of crofters dealing with coastal erosion by planting marram grass on dune systems.

Co-operatives: Lewis Crofters Ltd is the oldest co-operative on the Isle of Lewis. Founded in 1956 as a grass roots movement, it runs a store that stocks what the crofters need rather than items that give the most profit. *Co-chomunn*, or community co-operatives, are to be found in Barra, Vatersay, Harris and Lewis, as well as in the Uists. Some were set up by the Highlands and Islands Development Board, and each is different according to the local needs. Thus Co-chomunn an Lochdair Ltd (Carnan Stores) provides building, crofting and fishing supplies, while Keose Co-op in Lewis produces — among other things — organic fertilisers.

Craft Workshops: The Western Isles Craft Association (Breanish Pottery, 2 Breanish, Uig) can provide information about craft workshops in the islands. Hebridean Croft Originals at Lochboisdale, South Uist (4a West Kilbride) is a community-based business producing hand-framed knitwear, while traditional Harris tweed manufacture can be seen at Joan McLennan, Drinishadder, Harris, and Nesstex at Ness, Lewis (24 Swainbost).

Anti-Nuclear Initiatives: Stornoway airport is a strategic military staging post, though plans for a major expansion a few years ago were eventually shelved. Scotland Against Nuclear Dumping has a group in Lewis (6 Coll, Isle of Lewis).

Alternative Energy: Though there has been discussion about wind generation in the islands, nothing has so far appeared on the ground.

Transport: For information on ferries to the islands, contact Caledonian MacBrayne Ltd (The Ferry Terminal, Gourock). On Lewis, the public bus service operators are Loch Motors Ltd (Cameron Terrace, Leurbost) and Mrs M Mackay (1 Dalbeg) while on Harris services are operated by Harris Garage Coaches Ltd (Tarbert). On South Uist, services are provided by Hebridean Coaches Ltd (Howmore). Bike hire is available on Lewis from Alex Dan Cycle Centre (67 Kenneth Street, Stornoway) and The Sports Shop (6 North Beach Street, Stornoway), and on South Uist from Uist Cycle Cash and Carry (Old Telephone Exchange, Griminish).

Food: For places to eat, on Harris there is Scarista House, offering home-baking and free-range food, and Rosevilla Tearooms at Tarbert. Bread baked by traditional methods on the premises and other wholefoods can be bought in Stornoway from Matheson's (Francis Street). The Barra Community Co-op (Co-op office, Castlebay) sells wholefoods, and runs a tearoom at the airstrip.

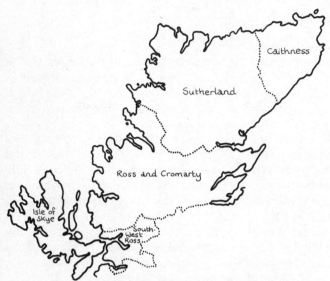

Caithness

Sutherland

Ross and Cromarty

Isle of Skye

South West Ross

North West Highlands

This, the largest of the ten regions in this book, is the most rugged and the least populated. In landscape terms the contrasts are violent — and the weather frequently offers similar variety. From the 'winged isle' of Skye with the volcanic Cuillins and the basalt columns of the Quiraing, through the great Torridonian sea cliffs of Wester Ross and the interminable barrens of Sutherland, to the rolling fertile farmlands of Dornoch and Caithness, this is

awe-inspiring country.

Rain and wind have had a marked effect on the vegetation of the region. Trees will simply not grow on the north coast west of the Kyle of Durness, though only seventy miles further south, at the head of a sheltered west-facing bay, are the renowned Inverewe Gardens, where palm trees flourish.

The glens of the north-west were not always as empty as they are today, for this area was the scene of some of the most brutal eighteenth and nineteenth century clearances. A visit to the little museum at Bettyhill, for example, will explain how Strathnaver supported several hundred families until it was cleared for sheep.

In many ways this is not an easy place to live even today. It could hardly be more beautiful, but distances are long and tiring when the local shop and school have closed and the postbus comes only once each day. Tourism is a vital industry here, enabling most communities to survive and some to thrive. The distance from urban centres has brought less wholesome activities too, like the white elephant fast breeder nuclear reactor at Dounreay and the bombing range at Cape Wrath, but there is still space enough to escape from the makebelieve world of towns and traffic to the real world of sea, wind, and some of the oldest rocks in the world.

Regional Tourist Offices: Caithness Tourist Board, Whitechapel Road, Wick, Caithness KW1 4EA (Tel: 0955 2596); Sutherland Tourist Board, The Square, Dornoch, Sutherland IV25 3SD (Tel: 0862 810400); Ross and Cromarty Tourist Board, Information Centre, North Kessock, Inverness IV1 1XB (Tel: 0463 73 505); Isle of Skye and South West Ross Tourist Board, Tourist Information Centre, Portree, Isle of Skye IV51 9BZ (Tel: 0478 2137).

Ancient Sites: Not to be missed in the north-west are the massive iron age brochs, round tower houses which once stood forty or fifty feet high. The best examples are Dun Telve and Dun Trodden, sited picturesquely in Gleann Beag, south of Glenelg, though you will also find ruined brochs as far east as Rangag and Ousdale in Caithness. Myth and early history are inextricably woven in many stories about the region's landmarks, but you can at least imagine the mermaids at Sandwood Loch, the devil tempting the seventeenth century wizard Lord Reay at the spectacular Smoo Caves, and the fairies donating their banner to the Macleods in an hour of need — the Fairy Flag (historians say it came from Rhodes in the seventh century) can still be seen in the drawing-room at Dunvegan Castle.

Trees and Woodland: As elsewhere in Scotland, uncontrolled conifer planting has ruined parts of the region and threatens to do yet more damage: currently at risk is the unique 'flow country' of Caithness. In the west and south of the region there is more mixed woodland, while native birch scrub woodland can still be seen in a few places, as at the Inchnadamph reserve in Sutherland.

Eight miles south of Ullapool, not far from the spectacular Corrieshalloch Gorge, is the Lael Forest Walk, a well-defined trail through a cross between a forest and an arboretum. Anyone confused by all the different conifers to be found in the area will find this walk very helpful, as key species are identified and named. At Gearchoille near Ardgay in Sutherland is one of Scotland's community-owned woodlands, owned and managed by the local community.

The Highlands Environmental Information Service (Duartbeg, Scourie, Sutherland) produces a fascinating magazine called *The Tree-Growers Guide to the Galaxy* which includes much detailed information about forestry in the region, and the Highlands Green Party has produced a very informative booklet about the *Ancient Forest of Caledon*.

Wildlife: Bare rock, peat and blanket bog cover most of the region, though around the coasts there is more variety of habitat. The shallow firths of the east attract huge numbers of wildfowl and waders, while the cliffs of the Sutherland reserve of Handa are home to large breeding populations of razorbill, kittiwake and fulmar. The mountains of Skye support rare alpine plants and breeding pairs of golden eagles. The Beauly Firth is one of the few places in Britain where dolphins may regularly be seen, and there have been calls to make it a marine nature reserve.

Between Brora and Helmsdale is a stone marking the spot where the last wild wolf in Scotland was reputedly killed, while by a rather gruesome coincidence the last witch to be burned alive in the country is commemorated by a slab in Littletown, Dornoch. The Wolf's Stone is dated 1700; the Witch's Stone 1722. The Skye Environmental Centre at Broadford runs a range of field courses and walking holidays; there is also a small natural history museum and a seal rescue centre, and you can stay there a night at a time as a B&B guest (good vegetarian food). A similar centre is the Waterstein Field Studies Centre at Oisgill House, Glendale.

Protected Areas: There are nearly twenty national nature reserves in the region, including the internationally renowned Beinn Eighe reserve displaying remnants of the original Caledonian pine forest (two nature trails, leaflet available from the Aultroy Visitor Centre) and the large Inverpolly reserve, where a range of moorland, mountain, woodland and coastal habitats are being conserved. Much of the coastline, including nearly all the western seaboard and the

Cuillin and Trotternish mountains on Skye, have been designated national scenic areas.

Access to the Countryside: Apart from the more intensively farmed eastern seaboard, you can walk almost anywhere you want to in the region, taking sensible precautions of course (the Scottish Tourist Board's *Hillwalking in Scotland* includes the Mountain Code as well as descriptions of the chief mountain ranges. As well as real hillwalking, several easier footpaths take you to places well worth the effort. These include the path to Culnacraig from Ardmair, just north of Ullapool, the walk along the Quiraing in northern Skye, and the Knockan Cliff Walk at Achiltibuie, where a wooden walkway winds its way around a cliff where rocks of vastly differing ages have been thrust over one another. If you like gardens, Inverewe is not to be missed, with its semi-tropical gardens overlooking The Minch.

If you would prefer to explore the north-west as part of an organised group, write to North-West Frontiers (19 West Terrace, Ullapool, Ross-shire) or Highland Contours (Rosslyn, Barbaraville, Delny, Ross-shire), who both offer a range of holidays from leisurely rambles to exhilarating hill walks.

Organic Initiatives: Not exactly organic, but certainly worth a visit if you are interested in novel ways of growing things, is the Hydroponicum alongside the Summer Isles Hotel in Achiltibuie. The Hydroponicum is a giant greenhouse which maximises input of solar energy to grow a wide range of exotic fruits, all the way from strawberries to bananas. There are regular guided tours during the tourist season. Again not quite organic, but producing exquisite wines including birch and elderflower, is the Moniack Winery at Moniack Castle, Kirkhill; as well as tastings and tours there is a pleasant little café.

At Craigs Farm, Plockton, near Kyle of Lochalsh, you can see a variety of rare breeds of farm animals.

Museums: Museums in Caithness worth visiting are the Laidhay Croft Museum near Helmsdale, the Wick Heritage Centre, and Thurso Folk Museum. Timespan at Helmsdale is yet another 'heritage centre', but picks out graphic scenes from the region's history; there is also a medicinal and culinary herb garden. Hugh Miller's Cottage in Cromarty, the birthplace of the famous Scottish geologist and now run by the National Trust for Scotland, is a picturesque thatched house with displays of the man's life and achievements. Another crofthouse folk museum can be found at Luib, on Skye between Broadford and Sligachan, while The Clan Donald Centre at Armadale — if you don't mind being where everyone else is — features an audio-visual display, restaurant, bookshop and craft shop; when you've had enough of that, you can walk in the woodland gardens or follow the nature trail.

Communal Groups: The peninsula opposite Ullapool, on the far side of Loch Broom, is home to one of the most interesting and undoubtedly green communities in Scotland — Scoraig. Originally a thriving crofting community, by the 1960s Scoraig had been abandoned, the main reason being that it has no road to it. Recolonisation started in the late 1960s, and although there is still no road nor mains services, it is now a strong and thriving community.

You can get to Scoraig by walking in from the hamlet of Badrallach, or by boat across the neck of Little Loch Broom from Badlaurach. Though there are no regular services, Scoraig residents — who you will most easily contact through places like the Ceilidh Place in Ullapool — will usually be happy to ferry you across.

Your first impression of Scoraig will be of tiny houses, some traditional crofts and some new houses (there is even a turf-covered dome) nestling among the folds of the hill, nearly all sporting a small wind generator — most of the village's electricity is generated in this manner. Despite its back-to-the-land feel, Scoraig is surprisingly high-tech. It also has the smallest secondary school on the British mainland, and a new schoolhouse is under construction.

Scoraig is not altogether happy as a tourist attraction. Since it was featured on television more and more tourists have started arriving, often expecting villagers to drop everything and spend the day explaining their philosophy; be sensitive. A small-scale tourist industry has developed, however: a wooden hut beside the primary school has been turned into a kitchen where visitors can buy drinks and snacks (proceeds to the school), and some crafts are also on sale. The building of a shop has recently started near the jetty.

Samadhan at Scoraig is a healing and holiday centre, created from a ruined crofthouse, where you can either take part in one of their organised events or just go for a retreat. Food is mostly home-grown organic vegetarian, but with local seafood and venison for treats. For details write to Samadhan at Scoraig, Dundonnell, by Garve, Wester Ross IV23 2RE.

With only a couple of tractors and several mountain bikes for transport, Scoraig moves at a different pace to the rest of Scotland, but this is as much a vision of the future as a return to the past.

Community Initiatives: Highland Forum (Woodside, Balblair, Dingwall) is a network for encouraging rural community initiatives throughout the Highlands; it produces a magazine called *The Bridge*. Skye Forum (Hazelmount, Viewfield Road, Portree) is a research group particularly interested in land use: they recently helped to produce a survey called *Rural Land Use of Skye*.

Co-operatives: One fascinating co-operative in this region is The Clown Jewels theatre group, who can be contacted at Grotaig, Bunloit, Drumnadrochit. The Clown Jewels travel the Highlands in a converted double decker bus, bringing their show — which often deals with controversial topics like nuclear dumping — to community halls and rural schools.

Craft Workshops: Founded as an innovative project by Sutherland County Council and the Highlands and Islands Development Board in 1964, Balnakeil Craft Village occupies the site of a former Ministry of Defence early warning station. Today it provides an excellent opportunity to see a wide range of craftworkers at their trades, with an opportunity to buy directly from the makers of candles, woodwork, patchwork wallhangings and much else.

At Fox Farm, Ardross, is the Weavers Workshop, where spinning, weaving and natural dyeing can be seen and the results bought. At Dornoch, the old town jail has been converted into an innovative craft centre, while the Victorian station at Strathpeffer has been adapted to create a series of tasteful craft shops and a small restaurant. Rhu Studio, three miles north of Ullapool, is an excellent art gallery where you can see (and buy if you want) vivid semi-abstract landscapes which are evocative of the area's wild scenery. At Broadford on Skye you can visit the Borealis shop, where the essential oils they make themselves (for massage and aromatherapy) can be purchased, while Ragamuffin at Armadale sells an imaginative range of knitwear and pottery, the products of local craftworkers.

Nuclear Energy and Anti-Nuclear Initiatives: If you want to see the inside of Britain's prototype fast breeder nuclear reactor at Dounreay, opened in 1957, tour tickets are available from the tourist information centre in Thurso or from the exhibition centre at the site; sometimes it is also possible to visit the nuclear waste store. The Caithness Campaign Against Nuclear Dumping can be contacted at 19 Smith Terrace, Wick. The Highland Anti-Nuclear Group (HANG) is very active, and can be contacted at West End, Milton, Drumnadrochit.

Alternative Energy: There is a 55kw Vestas wind generator near Golspie in Sutherland. A typical Caithness watermill has been restored at Westerdale, west of Wick.

Transport: A variety of operators run bus services in the region, and you shouldn't miss British Rail's 'north lines' from Inverness to Kyle of Lochalsh, Wick and Thurso. For full details of public tranport, buy a copy of *Getting Around the Highlands and Islands* (£2.50), available throughout the region. Bicycles can be hired in Gairloch (Glencairn Craft Shop, Strath Square) and North Kessock (Inverness Water Sports Centre, Coulmore Bay), and on Skye from Island Cycles

(Struan Road, Portree, and 7 Ebost, Struan). Mountain bikes can be hired from Rosehall Mountain Bikes, Invercassley Cottage, Rosehall, near Lairg; Assynt Mountain Bike Hire, Culag Buildings, Lochinver.

Health: Practitioners of alternative healing are very thin on the ground in the north-west; ask at The Ceilidh Place in Ullapool for details of visiting therapists.

Food: After years when it was impossible to find decent wholefoods in the area, the situation has now been transformed, with several restaurants providing an excellent and varied menu; many now serve very good vegetarian and vegan meals too. These include the Highland Designworks Wholefood Cafe at Plockton Road, Kyle of Lochalsh; The Dunnet Head Tearoom near Thurso; The Ceilidh Place and The Frigate Restaurant in Ullapool; Maggie's Cafe in Francis Street, Dornie; and several eating places on Skye: the Strathcorrie Restaurant at Broadford; The Three Rowans at Kildonan, Arnisort; The Green House at Struan; and The Three Chimneys at Colbost, near Dunvegan. An Greideal at Staffin in north Skye is run by the Staffin Community Co-operative. Wholefoods and organic vegetables can be bought in Cromarty from The Country Larder in the High Street.

Bookshops: The Ceilidh Place in Ullapool is an oasis for the green traveller: as well as being the best vegetarian restaurant/coffee shop/hotel in the area, there is a well-stocked bookshop, and live music in the summer. This is also the place to make contact with the West Highlands Peace Group. Achins Bookshop at Inverkirkaig, Lochinver, has a surprisingly large stock for its location; this is because it supplies most of the schools and colleges in the north of Scotland.

Local Directories: A sensible buy for any green-tinted traveller visiting the north-west is *The Vegetarian Guide to the Scottish Highlands*, 90p from bookshops and some craft shops. It lists more than 40 bed-and-breakfast establishments, centres and hotels, as far afield as Fort William, Aviemore and Elgin. If you are staying in the west of the region, make sure to pick up a copy of the *West Highland Free Press*, an independent, fearless and pioneering weekly newspaper, rare in a world of growing media empires.

The Great Glen

Straight as an arrow through the heart of the Highlands runs the Great Glen. Based on a massive geological fault, which more than twenty million years ago tore the ancient rocks apart and dragged the land on either side forty miles lengthwise, the Glen has always been an important route from east to west coasts.

At its eastern end lies the important administrative centre of Inverness, 'The Capital of the Highlands'. The town is a favourite tourist centre, and with the River Ness running through its heart and a backdrop of mountains has an airy feel. Inverness's hinterland is wooded and gently rolling, especially inland from Nairn where Macbeth's Cawdor Castle and the bleak battlefield of Culloden Muir are both much-visited.

Loch Ness continues to flourish on its monstrous legends, though the steep-sided glens to north and south are also worth exploring. Fort William is not a beautiful town and can be very crowded in summer, as can the main route up Ben Nevis, Britain's highest mountain. Further west, however, the country

becomes more open and barren, until by the time you reach the open sea around the Ardnamurchan peninsula you have left the trappings of mass tourism far behind.

Looking out from Ardnamurchan or from the Skye ferry terminal at Mallaig, you will see what are collectively called 'The Small Isles', more viewed from afar than visited. Rhum, the largest, is dominated by a cluster of spectacular peaks and ridges, relics of ancient volcanic activity; it is now one of the largest nature reserves in Scotland. Eigg, Muck and Canna are also striking, especially the former with its striking hexagonally columned rocks.

Regional Tourist Offices: Inverness, Loch Ness and Nairn Tourist Board, 23 Church Street, Inverness IV1 1EZ (Tel: 0463 234353); Fort William and Lochaber Tourist Board, Cameron Centre, Cameron Square, Fort William, Inverness-shire PH33 6AJ (Tel: 0397 3781).

Ancient Sites: The Nairnshire foothills east of Inverness are rich in archaeological sites, most notably the Clava Cairns near Culloden, an extensive group of bronze age cairns and standing stones. As well as being famed world-wide for its giant 'worm', a claim dating back to the seventh century at least, Loch Ness is also the setting for another well-known folk legend -that of the woman who saw the loch fill from an overflowing spring and exclaimed 'Tha loch an a nis' ('There's a lake in it now'), thus giving the newly-formed loch its name. Loch Morar, the deepest loch in Scotland, is also said to have its own monster: Castle Tioram, a picturesque ruin on an islet in Loch Moidart, is the ancient seat of the Clan Macdonald.

Trees and Woodland: The Forestry Commission has established a number of large plantations in the region, the most extensive in Glen Affric and to the south and east of Inverness. Many have nature trails and picnic facilities, including a 'Battlefield Trail' at Culloden and, for the more energetic, a ten-mile trail around Loch Affric. The native woodland which survives in the west is mainly birch, though in the east, particularly in the valleys of the Nairn and Findhorn Rivers, there are some magnificent beechwoods. At Balintraid, Delny, near Invergordon is a small organic tree nursery.

Wildlife: With the exception of some rich farmland close to the Moray Firth, the land in this region is used chiefly for sheep farming, forestry and shooting estates; thus grouse and deer are economically important forms of 'semi-wildlife'. Heather is predominant in the east, while the moorlands of the east are characterised by blanket bog supporting little more than sphagnum moss, moorgrass and cotton-grass. The high mountains are home to pretty alpine plants like the starry saxifrage and the Scottish asphodel, together with golden eagle, peregrine falcon and merlin. The influence of the sea is paramount in the west, particularly on the islands: the whole range of maritime habitats can be seen in the Rhum reserve. Despite some spectacular cliff scenery, seabird colonies are generally small, though Rhum is home to vast colonies of Manx shearwater and storm petrels nest on Canna.

Protected Areas: Much of the west of the region has been designated National Scenic Areas: The Small Isles; Morar, Moidart and Ardnamurchan; Loch Shiel; and Ben Nevis and Glencoe. The region's nature reserves include Claish Moss, a raised peat mire near Strontian, and Loch Sunart Woodlands with their mix of native trees and a rich variety of mosses. As well as being a national nature reserve, Rhum has also been designated an international Biosphere Reserve.

Access to the Countryside: Access to the countryside in most of the region is not difficult, though care should be taken on steep mountainsides. Nairnshire has some very attractive scenery on a less grand scale than the high mountains bordering the Great Glen: the walk to the Ardclach Belltower above the River Findhorn and the nearby riverside walks are especially delightful. Fort William is the northern terminus of The West Highland Way (for details see under 'Central Highlands').

Peace: At the summit of Ben Nevis is a peace monument, erected by a local minister.

Organic Initiatives: At Redhill Farm, Allanfearn, near Inverness organic oats and barley are grown, and sheep and cattle are raised to organic standard.

Museums: The Fishertown Museum in Nairn describes graphically how the community has changed over the years.

Communal Projects: The Fellowship of Life (Nirvana, 12 Argyle Street, Inverness) is a small Christian community dedicated to the promotion of cruelty-free living.

Co-operatives: An important new co-operative has recently opened for business in Inverness: this is Highland Wholefoods at 13 Harbour Road, who supply wholefoods to shops and consumer co-ops throughout the Highlands and Islands.

Craft Workshops: Culloden Pottery at Gollanfield near Nairn also has a pleasant gift shop and tearoom; on some days the public are invited to make their own pots. At the Culloden Moor Weaving Studio you can see weaving being done on traditional Scottish handlooms. Northern Lights at Firthside, Lentran, by Inverness is a workshop making and selling candles of all shapes and sizes, while at Kirkhill, south of Beauly, a former church has been converted to become the workshop of Highland Aromatics, where high quality hand-made soap is made.

Alternative Energy: At Lower Foyers on the south side of Loch Ness is the site of Britain's first hydro-electric power station, opened in 1896; the present scheme is a pumped storage operation, using Loch Mhor as a 'header tank'. At Mill of Tore, Balnain, is a restored eighteenth century meal mill.

Transport: For full details of public transport in the region, it is a good investment to buy a copy of *Getting Around the Highlands and Islands* (£2.50 from tourist information offices). The Caledonian Canal runs through the Great Glen from Inverness in the north to Corpach in the south. It is managed by the British Waterways Board, whose local office is at Clachnaharry Road, Inverness. The BWB employs a ranger, who looks after the interests of both wildlife and visitors. There are pleasant canalside walks along the canalised sections (more than two-thirds of the canal's length uses the natural Lochs Ness, Oich and Lochy); there are organised boat trips at the Inverness end, and boats can be hired from several places, including Dochgarroch on Loch Ness and the Great Glen Water Park on Loch Oich.

Cycles can be hired in Fort William from Lees Cycle Hire (Leesholme, Cameron Road) or Off Beat Bikes (4 Inverlochy terrace); also in Lochaber from Bespoke Highland Tours (The Bothy, Camusdarach, by Arisaig) and Scott Gunn (The Forestry Shed, Glen Nevis). In Inverness the places for cycle hire are Sharps in Station Square, Ness Motors in King Street and Academy Motors at 122 Academy Street, while the Loch Insh Watersports centre at Kincraig and the Glen Affric Hotel at Cannich also hire bicycles.

Health: At Tigh na Bruaich, Struy, by Beauly (Tel: 0463 76254) is Linda Christie's holistic therapy centre, offering healing and psychotherapy. For information about other practitioners in the area, you can either ring Linda or The Apothecary at The Findhorn Foundation (see 'Health' in the North-East section).

Food: I know of no specifically wholefood restaurants in the region, though Inverness has a few places where vegetarians and other healthy eaters will find a reasonable selection. These include Brookes Wine Bar (75 Castle Street), the Dickens International Restaurant (77-79 Church Street), the restaurant at the Eden Court Theatre in Bishops Road, where there are often exhibitions of local artists' work, and, if you want to treat yourself, Dunain Park Hotel, which prepares delicious dishes from local ingredients, including their own organic produce. Another hotel where eating is a healthy treat is the Clifton Hotel in Nairn; they too use organic homegrown vegetables and herbs, and can always cater for vegetarians and vegans. The restaurant at the Culloden Pottery, Gollanfield (between Inverness and Nairn) offers imaginative vegetarian dishes. The Health Shop at 20 Baron Taylors Street, Inverness, carries a reasonable range of wholefoods. In Fort William, the Nevisport Restaurant in the High Street is reasonable.

There are also several good vegetarian B&Bs in the region, including the Glendale Guest House in Invergarry (Mandally Road), the Brae Hotel in Fort Augustus, and Easter Dalziel Farm at Dalcross near Inverness.

Bookshops: County Books in Nairn is a very green-tinted small town bookshop with an imaginative stock; you will also be able to find out about green activities in the Nairn area here. Melvens' bookshop in Inverness is also making an effort. Charles Leakey's second-hand bookshop in Bank Street, Inverness, is by far the best in the Highlands.

Local Directories: Based in Nairn (PO Box 7) is Moray Firth Link, a local environmental information network. *The Vegetarian Guide to the Highlands* (90p from bookshops and tourist information centres) covers this region.

North East Scotland

Though there are many local differences in the north-east, there is a common character to the whole region. To the south and west are the high mountains, rising to over 4000 feet in the craggy Cairngorms. To the north and east is the sea, with fishing towns and villages crowding into coves or huddled against the wind around long curving bays. Between, in a strip never more than thirty miles wide and often much less, is the farmland which is still the region's chief economic mainstay.

There are places where the mountains are threatened with leisure developments (the wooden huts, car parks and eroded hillsides at The Lecht highlight the risk), but for the most part the peaks and the wide glens are still unspoilt in their grandeur. The coast, too, is largely free from the trappings associated with mass tourism, and a cliff walk such as that from Rosehearty to

Gardenstown is much as it was thirty years ago, village pubs and seaside cafés with real gingham tablecloths to boot.

I have included in this section the former county of Angus, now part of Tayside, since it shares many of the qualities of its northern neighbours. The richer farmland of Strathmore provides a livelihood for picturesque little market towns like Forfar, Kirriemuir, Brechin and Edzell, and the lowlands are fringed to the north-west by the highland boundary fault and lovely, lonely glens with evocative names like Glenisle and Glendoll, winding deeply into the hills.

The north-east has just as much to offer the discerning traveller, if not more, as the more tourist-frequented areas further to the west. From Scotland's largest and most impressive Pictish sculptured stone — Sueno's Stone at Forres — and an array of eighteenth century planned villages, to the impressive herb garden at Old Semeil and the striking Universal Hall at the Findhorn Foundation, there is sufficient here to fill many days of a green-tinted holiday.

ABERDEEN

'Boom'n'Bust-on-Dee' Aberdeen has been called, and the short-lived boom of North Sea oil is just the latest and biggest that the city has witnessed in its long history. But many things about Aberdeen have lived through all the city's economic vicissitudes and survived: most of its solid granite building, its dependence on the sea, its dogged determination and dark humour.

Save for the few at the top who worked hard to get there and then took advantage of their wealth, Aberdonians have historically always had to work hard for their living, labouring at sea, on the land, in the quarry, or at home with precious few conveniences. So for the most part they take the latest downturn stoically, secretly pleased that in many ways life can now return to normal. And as cities go Aberdeen is very normal, less a small city than a very large town. 'How can a town of two hundred thousand people survive so far north?' asks historian John Allan. 'Because,' he believes, 'it is completely relevant to the country it lives in.'

Like the other Scottish cities, though mercifully on a slightly smaller scale, Aberdeen has been mauled by postwar developers. The designers of the earlier suburbs, like Kincorth, still faced houses with granite, but by the early 1960s high-rises were the order of the day, 33 of them, dominating the city skyline. Developers are still at their ploys, one of the latest monstrosities being the George Street shopping centre, nicknamed Gulag by some locals. Now many of the new office developments lie empty, leaving the city council to devise ways of making them relevant to the city's needs.

While in Aberdeen, walk along the seafront or round the headland at Girdleness to remind yourself of the sea which is Aberdeen's *raison d'être*, and don't miss the neat and picturesque ex-fishing settlement at Footdee ('Fiddie' to the natives).

Tourist Information Office: St Nicholas House, Broad Street, Aberdeen AB9 1DE (Tel: 0224 632727).

Wholefood Restaurants: Aberdeen's only genuine wholefood restaurant is a co-operative venture called Jaws (5 West North Street); the menu is limited but perfectly adequate, and prices are reasonable. Two good fish restaurants (you are in Aberdeen . . .) are the Ashvale Fish Restaurant (46 Great Western Road) and the Silver Darling Restaurant (Pocra Quay, North Pier, Footdee).

Wholefood Shops: Aberdeen's truly green wholefood shop is Ambrosia Wholefoods, a worker's co-operative at 160 King Street. They carry a wide range, and send orders to customers all over the Highlands and Islands.

Bookshops: Bissets at 12-14 Upperkirkgate is Aberdeen's biggest bookshop; it has a small 'green' section. Aberdeen's radical bookshop is Boomtown Books (167 King Street), a small shop but with a good selection, especially on conservation and Scottish issues.

Museums: Of Aberdeen's half dozen museums, the two which are really worth a visit are the Maritime Museum at Provost Ross's House, Shiprow, where a sixteenth century shipmerchant's home now houses a display of seafaring artefacts and memorabilia, and the University of Aberdeen's Anthropological Museum in Broad Street, where you can learn a lot about the region's prehistory.

Shops and Crafts: Shopping in Aberdeen is pretty predictable, though two craft-cum-gift shops worth visiting for their range of Scottish crafts are Kist (37a Marischal Street) and Orrock Crafts (196 Rosemount Place). Aberdeen's Third World Centre at St Mary's Chapel, Correction Wynd, sells crafts, 'fair trade' tea and coffee, recycled paper products and a small selection of wholefoods. Markets are held on Fridays and Saturdays on The Green, and on Fridays in Justice Street (if the weather allows).

City Wildspaces: Aberdeen's city farm is at Doonies Farm, Cove, alongside Loirston Country Park (booklet available), where you can walk along the clifftop. Hazelhead Gardens and the Cruikshank Botanic Gardens offer more manicured natural surroundings, while Brimmond and Elrick Country Park, in the hills to the north-west of the city (booklet available) has moorland walks and views over Aberdeen and its surroundings. The disused Deeside railway line has been made into a very pleasant footpath, accessible at Duthie Park or Auchinyell Road. The natural history of Aberdeen has been carefully studied by Peter Marren, who has written a book of that name which is obtainable in Aberdeen bookshops.

Transport: It isn't easy to find out about public transport in Aberdeen; tourist information seems more willing to tell you about car hirers — an effect of the oil boom? But buses there are, and the bus station in Guild Street will be able to provide details. Bicycles can be hired in Aberdeen from Aberdeen Cycle Centre (188 King Street).

Community Initiatives: Information about community arts activities in Aberdeen can be obtained from Peacock Printmakers, who run Artspace at 21 Castle Street. Artspace shows a wide range of exhibitions in three galleries, as well as organising touring shows.

The Camphill Community at Newton Dee Village, Bieldside, provides an environment in which able-bodied and handicapped people work and live together: there is a large organic garden and the community also produces a range of craft items.

The Aberdeen Urban Studies Centre (Skene Square School, 61 Skene Square) is an environmental resource centre for the city. The Centre produces a local recycling guide and a range of other publications, and is also the home of the Aberdeen Urban Wildlife Group. Aberdeen Civic Society, the city's foremost civic amenities group, is at Windsor Park, Kinellar.

Co-operatives: There are now more than a dozen workers' co-operatives trading in Aberdeen, including a number of specialist technical support firms as well as the expected craft and wholefood businesses. The Scottish Co-operatives Development Committee's local office (Aberdeen Business Centre, Willowbank House, Willowbank Road) will be able to supply full details.

Peace: Peace groups in Aberdeen can be contacted through the Third World Centre (see under 'Shops and Crafts'). A Japanese peace garden has been established in Duthie Park. Aberdeen Peace Centre is at 15 Belmont Street Aberdeen (Tel: 0224 648883).

Health: Aberdeen has no natural health centre, though there are a number of practitioners working in the city. For details, the Institute of Complementary Medicine's local information number is 033 022 164.

Local Directories: Aberdeen and Grampian Environmental Database Directory (Grampian Regional Council Education Department Resource Centre, Belmont Street) is part of the education service of Grampian Regional Council, and can provide a wide range of local information.

DUNDEE

Dundee tends to get bypassed by many holiday-makers, which is a pity, because despite having tried very hard to destroy its fabric and character with bulldozers and concrete the city has a lot to recommend it. The horrible Stakis Hotel and the dreary Tayside Regional Council headquarters, not to mention the tangle of roads leading to the Tay Road Bridge, have all but destroyed Dundee's once-picturesque waterfront, though the current redevelopment at Discovery Quay may improve things a little.

The river is what made Dundee, with Tay-built ships helping to turn the late nineteenth century city into the world's jute capital. Seville oranges brought by ship from Spain and local berries from the rich farms of Strathmore and the Carse of Gowrie gave Dundee its renowned tradition of marmalade and jam making, while the local Thompson family turned Dundee into Scotland's focus for popular and demagogic journalism.

Dundee's position between the sea and the Sidlaw Hills, with the rolling Fife countryside just across the river, make the city a pleasant place to live, work, and visit. Climb to the top of Dundee Law, only minutes from the city centre, and on a clear day you will see Tayside spread out around you, splendid natural setting, man-made warts and all.

Tourist Information Office: 4 City Square, Dundee DD1 3BA (Tel: 0382 27723).

Wholefood Restaurants: Dundee's only real wholefood restaurant is Brambles (175 Brook Street, Broughty Ferry — a bus or train ride from the city centre); other restaurants offering decent vegetarian options include Raffles (18 Perth Road) and the Town House (1 King Street).

Wholefood Shops: The best of the city's wholefood shops is Dundee Wholefoods at 10 Perth Street, though there are a number of more mainstream health food shops such as Bon Appetit at 181 Perth Road and Tayside Health Foods at 42-44 Commercial Street.

Bookshops: Dundee's two best bookshops are James Thin (City Square) and the University Bookshop (95 Nethergate), both with small 'green' sections.

Museums: McManus Galleries in Albert Square is Dundee's principal museum and art gallery, featuring displays about local life and industry and a lively programme of craft workshops open to the public. The Mills Observatory in Balgay Park often runs astronomy workshops, while Discovery Quay, with Scott's (of the Antarctic) *Discovery* and the 150-year-old frigate *Unicorn* on display, is worth a visit. Dundee Heritage Trust is planning to convert a disused jute mill into an innovate visitor centre in the near future.

Shops and Crafts: Dundee shopping is adequate but not exciting. Two workshops worth visiting, however, are the Printmakers Workshop at the Seagate Gallery (38-40 Seagate) and Meadowmill Studios at West Henderson's Wynd.

City Wildspaces: Dundee is fortunate in having several country parks nearby. Camperdown Park, little more than two miles northwest of the city centre, provides Dundonians with acres of parkland and woodland to roam in (don't miss the Camperdown Elm), while the centrepiece of nearby Clatto Park is its reservoir, visited by hundreds of migrating waterbirds. Baldragon Wood and Templeton Woods offer woodland walks, while a little further afield are Monikie and Crombie Country Parks.

Transport: Cycles can be hired from Mac Cycles, 143c Nethergate, and mountain bikes from Boddens Mountain Equipment, 104 Annfield Road. There are several schemes for cycleways and footpaths in the city: the route from Kindgoodie and Invergowrie to Monifeith is being constructed, while there are long-term plans for a city-wide network. Tay Cycle Action Group can be contacted at 11 Crichton Street, Dundee DD1 3SP.

Energy Initiatives: Heat Development Dundee (Lower Dens Works, Princes Street) is part of the Britain-wide Heatwise initiative designed to provide local resources for energy conservation projects.

Community Initiatives: The city is proud of its tradition of supporting public art through the Dundee Public Arts Programme (36-40 Seagate): throughout the city you will come across murals, sculptures and innovative landscape features such as Keith Donnelly's ceramic panels in Bellfield Street and a gable end in St Peter Street depicting city life, painted by an artists' collective.

Dundee Tree Group (11 Killin Avenue) is very active, organising tree planting and environmental improvement projects. The Dundee

Urban Wildlife Project (Dundee Museum, Barratt Street) has conducted a survey of wildlife sites in the city.

Co-operatives: Until very recently Dundee had only one co-operative, Breadline Bakery, but since the establishment of a Dundee office of the Scottish Co-operatives Development Committee (Unit 9, Meadow Mill, West Henderson's Wynd; further information from them) in 1988 several new co-operatives have been established, including a furnishing business and a design studio.

Peace: There is a peace garden at Albert Square, and Dundee City Council has declared the city a nuclear-free zone.

Health: Though there are several practitioners of complementary medicine in the city, Dundee does not have a natural health centre.

Local Directories: *What's On* is a useful free quarterly publication produced by Dundee City Council, listing a wide range of activities from children's theatre to guided country walks.

THE REST OF THE REGION

Regional Tourist Offices: Moray District Council, 17 High Street, Elgin, Moray IV30 1EG (Tel: 0343 2666); Banff and Buchan Tourist Board, Collie Lodge, Banff AB4 1AU (Tel: 026 12 2789); Gordon District Tourist Board, St Nicholas House, Broad Street, Aberdeen AB9 1DE (Tel: 0224 632727); Kincardine and Deeside Tourist Board, 45 Station Road, Banchory, Kincardineshire AB3 3XX (Tel: 033 02 2066); Angus Tourist Board, Market Place, Arbroath, Angus DD11 1HR (Tel: 0241 77883).

Ancient Sites: There are hillforts atop many of the peaks in the region, such as those on Bennachie ('the mountain of light'), Dinnideer and Tap o' Noth, but the region's speciality is Pictish symbol stones, for this is the heart of the iron age kingdom of 'the painted people'. The Picts left little but several hundred incised stones and a tantalising set of 'king-lists', from which archaeologists and anthropologists have pieced together a picture of a settled people who chronicled their generations through the female line. Anthony Jackson's *The Pictish Trail* explains the intricacies of Pictdom, at the same time providing an itinerary which will take you to all the major monuments. Fyvie and Duffus castles are both the scenes of supernatural whirlwinds — 'fairy eddies' — while Glamis Castle is supposed to have one more window on the outside than can be accounted for from the inside: my favourite of the various explanations is that Earl Beardie is still in there playing cards with the devil. The Culbin Sands near Forres, which apparently engulfed another nobleman in the middle of a card game in their relentless march across the landscape, have now been stabilised by a massive tree planting programme.

Trees and Woodland: The Forestry Commission has planted large conifer stands in many parts of the region, though there has been a considerable effort, as at Darnaway and Roseisle in Morayshire, to make them as visitor-friendly as possible. At Glen Tanar near Ballater (visitor centre with exhibition) is the most easterly, and possibly the finest, remnant of the original Caledonian pine forest which once clothed the Grampian mountains, while nearby is Dinnet Oakwood, one of the few of the region's remaining oak woodlands. The river valleys of Banff and Moray shelter impressive stretches of mature mixed woodland, which can be seen in a wild and wonderful natural setting at Randolph's Leap south of Forres (sometimes unwittingly renamed 'Gandalf's Leap' by groups of spiritual seekers from the nearby Findhorn Foundation). The Foundation (see under 'communal groups') runs tree planting schemes, and publishes the annual *Trees for Life Calendar*.

Wildlife: The desolate tops of the Cairngorms are one of Britain's few remaining semi-wilderness areas, and are of international importance. The climate is truly arctic, and the plants and animals found here — trailing azalea, cloudberry, mountain hare and snow bunting — attract the attention of many naturalists. The coastline is the other main attraction, especially for birdwatchers. The cliff at Fowlsheugh, between Stonehaven and Inverbervie, is home to 80,000 pairs of six seabird species, notably guillemots and kittiwakes, while the reedbeds of the Firth of Tay and the almost landlocked Montrose Basin are home to large flocks of waders, ducks and geese.

Protected Areas: Of the seven national nature reserves in the region, one — the Cairngorm Lochs — is also an internationally renowned RAMSAR wetland site. Deeside and the Cairngorms are also designated National Scenic Areas.

Access to the Countryside: Walking in the north-east is not difficult as long as you avoid Aberdeen-Angus bulls, standing crops and barbed wire. The region boasts no fewer than three long-distance paths: The Speyside Way from Spey Bay to Tomintoul with a spur to Dufftown railway station (leaflets from the Speyside Way Visitor Centre, Boat of Fiddich, Craigellachie); The Buchan Walkway along the disused Buchan railway line (this footpath is still being created, though the stretch near the Aden country park has been surfaced and the Ellon-Maud section is passable); and the West Gordon Way from Inverurie to Rhynie (leaflet from Gordon District Council, Blackhall Road, Inverurie). The local tourist boards have produced a booklet called *Hillwalking in the Grampian Highlands*, 85p from tourist information offices.

Several activity holiday centres in the region offer guided walking tours, including Highland Activity Holidays in Dufftown (25 Hillside Avenue), Hiking and Biking Scotland in Inverurie (Bogfur, Inverurie), Wild Land Guides at Insch (New Leslie Cottage, Leslie, by Insch), and Tramp the Gramps at Aboyne (Tabarro Ltd, 6 Stableyard Cottages, Glen Tanar).

Organic Initiatives: The region is known the world over for its Aberdeen-Angus beef, and several beef raisers have recently started experimenting with humanely-reared organically-fed cattle. Near Turriff, south of Banff, are two such farms, both with Soil Association recognition: Sawmill Croft at Forglen and Blakehouse at Crudie.

There is a long tradition of growing herbs in Scotland, partly because more showy plants are harder to cultivate. High in the Grampians at Strathdon is Old Semeil Herb Garden, established in 1981, where over a hundred different herbs are grown organically. You can buy herb plants and dried herbs at Old Semeil. There are also more-or-less organic herb gardens at The Old Manse, Bridge of Marnoch, near Huntly; Cranloch near Elgin (Cascade Nursery); and Kildrummy Castle near Alford.

Museums: There are several rural heritage museums in the region which give a good idea of the almost forgotten world of classics like Grassic Gibbons' *A Scots Quair*: the best are the Heritage Centre at Aden Country Park, Mintlaw; the Museum of Farming Life at Pitmedden, between Ellon and Oldmeldrum; the Angus Folk Museum at Kirkwynd near Forfar; and the small museums at Fochabers and Tomintoul. The Buckie Maritime Museum explains the history of the local fishing industry, as does the Arbuthnott Museum in Peterhead. The Ice House at Tugnet, Spey Bay, was the largest ice store in Scotland, built to keep the local salmon industry supplied with vital ice right through the summer.

Communal Groups: Anybody interested in intentional communities will be making a bee-line for Findhorn where, since its foundation in 1962, the Findhorn Foundation has steadily been spreading its wings. Based around an organic garden and a full programme of creative and spiritual workshops, this community of more than two hundred residents welcomes thousands of people each year, from casual visitors who are welcome to join the two-hour guided tour each afternoon to those who stay for three months or more. For a brochure about Findhorn's guest programme write to The Park, Findhorn, Forres, Morayshire IV36 0TZ.

The main part of the community inhabits a caravan park near the seaside village of Findhorn. Here you should make a point of visiting the Trading Centre and the Apothecary (natural healing remedies and tasty teas!), and the Universal Hall, a beautiful and versatile five-sided building housing a recording studio and an art gallery as well as a large auditorium (a public theatre and film programme is arranged during the summer). Don't miss the house at nearby Pineridge built out of half an old whisky barrel, and take a peek at the tree nursery and the weaving and pottery studios.

On the other side of the road into Findhorn village is Minton House, a healing and retreat centre (Minton House, Findhorn, Morayshire IV36 0YY), and the community also owns Station House in the village, where there is a sauna and healing room.

In Forres is Cluny Hill College, an ex-hotel where most workshop guests to the Foundation stay. Another half mile out of Forres on the Dallas road is Newbold House, a residential community of 35 people affiliated to the Foundation which also runs a residential workshop programme on spiritual themes (St Leonard's Road, Forres IV36 0RE).

At Pluscarden, in a peaceful and beautiful wooded valley south of Elgin, is a Benedictine monastery rebuilt in the 1950s. The monks grow much of their own food, and by advance arrangement you can stay at the abbey's retreat centre — women and men in the summer but men only in the winter (Pluscarden Abbey, Elgin IV30 3UA).

Community Initiatives: Upper Donside Community Trust is a particularly active community organisation which has produced an attractive guide to this dramatically picturesque part of the Grampian highlands: 'This is our valley,' they say, 'and we've prepared this leaflet ourselves to show our pride in it.' The Trust also organises an annual summer arts festival called Strathfest.

Co-operatives: The four co-operative businesses in the region include Grampian Organic Wine at Banchory, and a company making furniture out of recycled whisky barrels at Keith in Banffshire.

Craft Workshops: The region has a thriving and expanding craft industry with many craftworkers practising traditional skills using local materials and products. New skills and techniques have also been developed, while some of the heritage crafts in danger of extinction have been re-established. The North-East of Scotland Development Agency (8 Albyn Place, Aberdeen) has produced *Grampian Select Crafts*, listing local craftspeople whose work is of high standard and imaginative design. Wood workshops in the area can be found at Wild Wood Turnery (Craigston Castle, Turriff), Touch Wood Turnery (Old Mills, Old Mills Road, Elgin), and at Richard Brockbank's studio (Bay Cottage, Findhorn) where you can work alongside Richard on your own project. In Gardenstown, try the Harbour Workshop for hand-framed knitwear and local and maritime crafts, while at New Pitsligo, 4C's (a community-operated craft shop at 70 High Street) sells a variety of traditional local crafts including New Pitsligo lace. Russell Gurney Weavers (Brae Croft, Muiresk, Turriff) make and sell handwoven fabrics and products in natural fibres; they also give demonstrations and run residential weaving and spinning courses. The Scottish Sculpture Workshop (Lumsden, Huntly) is a charitable organisation run by artists themselves, providing workshop space for artists in wood, metal and stone. They have a small permanent outdoor exhibition, The Sculpture Walk, where you can see pieces of work that have been produced in the workshops.

Anti-Nuclear Initiatives: Banff Against Nuclear Dumping (BAND) can be contacted at West Croft, Sunnyside of Lethenty, Fyvie, Turriff.

Alternative Energy: At The Park, Findhorn (alongside the Findhorn Foundation) is Weatherwise Solar, a pioneering business in the supply and maintenance of low energy systems, mostly for private houses: you can see one of their installations on the roof of the Foundation's community centre. Just south of Aberdeen is a 60kw Palenko wind generator, installed in 1982.

On the River Isla in Angus is the Mill of Towie, still producing oatmeal in the traditional way using water power. Visitors are welcome, as they are at the Oldmills Visitor Centre in Elgin, where the River Lossie drives a working meal mill. A third watermill, a 200-year-old meal mill, is currently being restored at Sandhaven near Rosehearty.

Transport: In general, public transport in the region is well supported and well publicised; several innovative schemes like the Heatherhopper and Speyside Rambler have recently been introduced. Grampian Regional Council has a Public Transport Unit (Woodhill House, Westburn Road, Aberdeen) which promotes the use of public transport in the area. Together with local district councils, it supports a wide variety of bus and rail services. Information on routes, times and travel pass schemes can be obtained from tourist information offices in the region.

For cycle hire in Moray, Moray District Council has produced a leaflet called *Cycle and Mountain Bike Hire* in Moray, available from local tourist information offices. In Banff and Buchan, cycles can be hired in Peterhead (Robertson Sports, 1-3 Kirk Street, Peterhead), while in Gordon they are available from Huntly Cycle Centre (7 Granary Street, Huntly), Gartly Cycles (Station Cottage, Gartly) and from Haughton House Country Park at Alford. Further south in Kincardine and Deeside, the Huntley Arms Hotel in Aboyne hires out ordinary cycles as do A.J. Stewart (The Square, Tarland), Hamish Paterson (Bridge Street, Tarland) and the Riverside Garage (Tullich Road, Ballater). Mountain bike hire is available from Gairnsheil

Lodge (Glen Cairn, Ballater) and the Braemar Outdoor Centre (15 Mar Road, Braemar).

Cycle touring holidays in the region are organised by Hiking and Biking Scotland, Bogfur, Inverurie, and by Flycycle Holidays, 8 The Square, Cullen.

Health: Several practitioners of alternative healing methods are based in and around the Findhorn Foundation: ask at The Apothecary for details (Tel: 0309 31044). The Institute for Complementary Medicine public information number for the region is 033 022 164.

Food: For the time being, Findhorn seems to be the only source of wholefoods in the region, with a wholefood cafe at The Apothecary and a shop, The Trading Centre (both at The Park, Forres), which sells a good range of wholefoods. Elsewhere a few eating places advertise vegetarian meals as part of their menus. These include The Coffee Shop (8 South College Street) and the Sunninghill Hotel (Hay Street), both in Elgin, The Tollbooth Restaurant on the Old Pier at Stonehaven Harbour, and the Gordon Arms at Kincardine O'Neil.

Bookshops: The one green bookshop in the region is The Trading Centre at the Findhorn Foundation, which carries a wide range of titles on environmental, health and spiritual topics; it also issues a regular catalogue (The Trading Centre, The Park, Findhorn, Morayshire IV36 0TZ).

The Central Highlands

Except for the south-east corner of this region, where the rolling hills of Strathearn and Strathallan reach down to the headwaters of the Forth and Tay, this is a land of windswept, towering summits, steepsided glens and picturesque lochs. Parts of it have been ruined by tourist development — the ski resort of Aviemore, for example, is a place best avoided by the sensitive traveller, The Trossachs can be worse than Princes Street on a hot summer weekend, and the main track up Ben Lomond from Rowardennan is cracking up under the strain of thousands of hiking boots. The military have commandeered most of the region's short coastline along Loch Long and Loch Fyne, while Glen Douglas is a

87

large-scale weapons dump and Glen Fruin a testing site for torpedoes and other weaponry.

Yet large areas are now protected from unwanted development by National Scenic Area legislation, and there is wonderful hillwalking in the mountains of Atholl and Breadalbane. The heartland of Perthshire, where Ben Lawers and Ben Vorlich look down on Loch Earn and Loch Tay, is like a miniature Scottish Lake District, while if you can manage to see them without the company of a hundred other visitors, the Falls of Tummel and the Pass at Killiecrankie are quite awe-inspiring.

The charming towns of Stirling and Perth, both claiming the title of 'gateway to the Highlands' and both now relieved of through traffic by encircling motorways, act as the major centres for the southern part of the region, while sleepy, attractive market centres like Crieff and Callander have to a large extent become dormitories for the larger towns.

When in the Central Highlands take time to explore the sideroads. It's almost too easy to head north up the dual carriageway of the A9 and be in Inverness before you feel hungry. Almost every glen has a small sideroad which passes white-painted crofthouses, waterfalls and remnants of woodland before turning into a track, then into a footpath, then climbing the glen where only hardy hikers and the Range Rovers of shooting parties ever penetrate.

And, when walking the shores of Loch Lomond, remember that it was the glen at Inversnaid that inspired the poet Gerard Manley Hopkins to write 'Let them be left, the wildness and wet; long live the weeds and the wilderness yet.'

Regional Tourist Offices: Aviemore and Spey Valley Tourist Board, Grampian Road, Aviemore, Inverness-shire PH22 1PP (Tel: 0479 810363); Perthshire Tourist Board, The Round House, Marshall Place, Perth PH2 8NU (Tel: 0738 27958); Loch Lomond, Stirling and Trossachs Tourist Board, 41 Dumbarton Road, Stirling FK8 2LQ (Tel: 0786 75019).

Ancient Sites: Hill forts such as Dun da Lamh on a hilltop near Dalwhinnie are the most obvious early monuments in the region, though it is better known for its castles and tower houses than for its ancient sites. The region also has some impressive Pictish symbol stones, notably those at Logierait near Ballinluig and the Dupplin Cross south-west of Perth: for full details read section 4 of Anthony

Jackson's *The Pictish Trail* (Orkney Press, £3.95). 'The Stone of Scone,' one eminent historian has written, 'is, apart from Stonehenge, perhaps the most powerfully evocative object in these islands.' The Stone of Destiny, it is said, originally came from Spain, whence it came via Ireland to Scotland, to become the stone upon which all Scottish monarchs were crowned. In the thirteenth century it was built into a chair and installed in Westminster Abbey in London, but a raiding party of Scottish nationalists brought it back to Scotland in 1950. Many say that though a similar stone was surrendered to the authorities the following year, it was in fact a replica and the original Stone of Scone remains in Scotland. Though the Stone is no longer at Scone, the Palace at Scone is well worth visiting; the present palace is the third on the site, which has dark age and Pictish associations.

Trees and Woodland: Remnants of the original Forest of Caledon can be seen at the carefully managed sites at Abernethy Forest, Boat of Garten, and the Black Wood at Loch Rannoch. Apart from the shores of Loch Ard, Loch Katrine and the southern end of Loch Lomond, where the Queen Elizabeth Forest Park was created in 1956, the Forestry Commission has limited its activity in this region — and even here the planting is generally in keeping with the landscape. Britain's tallest hedge is to be found at Meikleour, twelve miles north of Perth; this fine beech hedge, planted in 1746, is 85 feet high and more than 600 yards long. On the Arden House Estate near Balloch is an organic tree nursery called The Trees Company.

The Scottish Community Woods Campaign, an organisation which promotes community ownership and management of native woodlands, is based in Aberfeldy (3 Kenmore Street), and there is an active local Tree Group in Blair Atholl (Loch Garry Tree Group, Berbice, The Terrace, Blair Atholl). Growing Up With Trees (also at 3 Kenmore Street, Aberfeldy) is a group which works with children, showing them how to look after trees and woodlands. The World Natural Rainforest Appeal is based in Perth (20f Ainslie Gardens, Muirton).

Countryside: The Countryside Commission for Scotland has its headquarters at Battleby, Redgorton, near Perth, where you can look round the visitor centre; the commission can also provide information on a wide range of Scottish environmental issues. The Kindrogen Field Centre at Enochdhu, Blairgowrie, runs a wide range of courses on environmental and natural history topics. Save the Cairngorms Campaign, PO Box 39, Inverness is an alliance of groups working to protect the Cairngorm Mountains from unsightly and damaging developments; it produces a regular newsletter.

Access to the Countryside: Excellent hillwalking can be found throughout the region: the Scottish Tourist Board's *Hillwalking in*

The Central Highlands

Scotland describes such highlights as Ben Lawers and Schiehallion, Ben Macdui and Cairngorm. Do take sensible precautions if you plan a long hill walk: the mountain code is reproduced at the beginning of the STB handbook. The southern — and easiest — section of the West Highland Way passes through the western edge of the region on its way from Milngavie in Strathclyde to Fort William in the Great Glen. A leaflet is available from the Countryside Commission for Scotland, and there is also an official handbook, *The West Highland Way* (HMSO, £6.95), which includes the necessary 1:50,000 Ordnance Survey maps.

There is a whole network of walks and trails in the Garry/Tummel area west of Pitlochry: an attractive guidebook is available from Pitlochry tourist information centre. Of the many excellent short walks in the region, three to be particularly recommended are the island nature reserve of Inchcailloch in Loch Lomond (boat service from Balmaha), the River Braan Walk near Dunkeld (which passes the tallest Douglas fir in Britain, over 200 feet high), and the spectacular Falls of Bruar, three miles west of Blair Atholl. The Countryside Ranger Service organises a comprehensive programme of guided walks in the region; ask for a leaflet at any tourist information office. Ossian Guides at Sanna, Newtonmore, organise walking tours to suit all abilities in the Cairngorm mountains.

Wildlife: The high mountain tops have been least disturbed by human influence, and here the springy alpine turf and rock ledges provide a paradise for botanists. Ben Lawers, a national nature reserve, is famed for its alpine-arctic flora. Here too you can see soaring golden eagles and watch ptarmigan play hide-and-seek.

The many small lochs in the south of the region are often spectacular for the thousands of grey geese which roost on winter evenings: Loch Leven is internationally important, with the Vane Farm Nature Centre adjacent to it. The Loch of the Lowes near Dunkeld is another important reserve, famous for its ospreys and great crested grebes. Loch Garten, too, is famous for its ospreys, while wanderers from the beaten track may well hear a crossbill extracting seeds from the cones of native pines or the scratching of a squirrel's claws.

Lakeside reserves like the Endrick mouth at the south end of Loch Lomond are the winter home for large flocks of wildfowl, while Flanders Moss to the west of Stirling is the largest raised valley bog in Britain, supporting a host of rare insects and a huge gull colony.

Protected Areas: Of the seven national nature reserves in the region, Rannoch Moor is also a designated RAMSAR wetland site of international importance. Much of the region falls within National Scenic Areas, including the Cairngorms, Loch Tummel, Loch Rannoch and Glen Lyon, Loch Lomond, The Trossachs, and part of Strathearn.

Organic Initiatives: There are nearly a dozen organic farms and smallholdings in Perthshire: Muirhall Farm near Perth specialises in 'natural lamb', while Jamesfield Farm near Abernethy is the location of a pioneering organic scheme where several agricultural agencies and a supermarket chain, Safeway, have helped to create an Organic Farming Centre (for details write to The Edinburgh School of Agriculture, West Mains Road, Edinburgh EH9 3JG). Other organic farms in the region specialise in pigs, vegetables and potatoes.

Museums: The Highland Folk Museum at Kingussie offers a fascinating insight into the working and living conditions of Highlanders over the last few centuries by means of reconstructed dwelling houses and mills, while at the Highland Tryst Museum in Crieff (Burrell Street) you can see a reconstructed weaver's house and demonstrations of handloom weaving. Landmark near Carrbridge exhibits some of the worst and the best of the new breed of heritage centres: go when tourists are thin on the ground to enjoy the treetop walk and the 'multivision show with three pairs of computer-controlled projectors and stereo sound' — it is actually rather good.

Co-operatives: Co-operatives are thin on the ground in this region, though the Scottish Co-operatives Development Committee now has an office in Stirling (The Resource Centre, Corn Exchange Road). Whinwell Weavers provides a marketing and retail service for small craft businesses throughout central Scotland, with a retail outlet near Stirling Castle, while The Lunch Bunch is a recently-founded catering co-op, also based in Stirling.

Craft Workshops: Highland Pottery (Church Terrace, Newtonmore) is a small craft pottery where you can see pots being hand-thrown, or have a go yourself at Barbara Davidson's Pottery (Muirhall Farm, Larbert) or at Loch-an-Eilein Pottery in Rothiemurchus. The focal point of the Mill Heritage Trail in Tillicoultry (Upper Mill Street) is the Clock Mill Centre, where craftspeople including weavers and coppersmiths can be seen at work. You can also see various crafts being demonstrated at the Bennybeg Craftworks Co-operative in Crieff (Muthill Road); they have a shop there too. There are demonstrations of the spinner's craft at the Yardspinners Workshop (Willoughby Street, Muthill). Handmade shoes and sandals are made at Edinample Shoes in Lochearnhead (South Loch Earn Road).

Energy Initiatives: At Pitlochry the River Garry has been dammed to form Loch Faskally, just one of a series of hydro-electricity schemes built in the Garry/Tummel catchment area; a display and exhibition inside the Pitlochry station explains how the system works, while the salmon ladder fascinates many visitors as the fish leap their way upstream. On a much smaller scale, a traditional meal mill has been restored at Blair Atholl, while Lower City Mills at West Mill Street,

Perth, is powered by Scotland's largest working waterwheel (pleasant tearoom, too). Heatsave in Stirling (Unit 46, Stirling Enterprise Park) is an organisation which provides information and practical assistance for energy conservation projects in the region.

Transport: For detailed information about public transport services in the region buy a copy of *Getting Around the Highlands and Islands* (£2.50 from tourist information offices). Ask about the Special Rover Ticket offered by Strathtay Scottish Omnibuses. Midland Scottish (Goosecroft Bus Station, Stirling) run bus services covering the Loch Lomond, Stirling and Trossachs region. The Central Highlands are reasonably well served by rail services, with the main Inverness line running through the heart of the region and the West Highland line serving Crianlarich and the remote outpost of Rannoch.

There is plenty of choice when it comes to hiring bikes in the Cairngorms. Children's bikes, tandems, tricycles and baby seats are available from some places, and the following firms hire out mountain bikes, an obvious choice in this area: Inveruglas Mountain Bike Adventures (Inveruglas, Insh, Kingussie), Inverdruie Mountain Bikes (Rothiemurchus Visitor Centre, Inverdruie), Red Mac Ski School (Red McGregor Hotel Car Park, Main Road, Aviemore), Wade Road Mountain Bikes (Slochd Nordic Ski School, Slochd, Carrbridge) and Sports Hire (Nethybridge). For ordinary bikes there are also Logans Bike Hire (Crann-Tara Guest House, High Street, Grantown-on-Spey), Norwest Sports Hire (Main Street, Newtonmore) and Loch Insh Watersports Centre (Insh Hall, Kincraig). In the south of the region, the tourist information centre at Callander hires out bikes, as do Trossachs Cycle Hire (Trossachs Holiday Park, Aberfoyle), Stewart Wilson Cycles (49 Barnton Street, Stirling), R.S. Finnie Cycles (Leadenflower Garage, Crieff) and the Ski Snow Shop (62 South Street, Perth).

Cycle tour holidays are organised by Scottish Cycling Holidays (Post Office, Ballintuim, Blairgowrie) and Highland Cycle Tours (Kincraig). The Glasgow-Loch Lomond Cycleway runs north from Dumbarton to the Loch alongside the River Leven, and other long-distance cycleways are being created, such as a route from Perth to Inverness paralleling the busy A9 road. Many Forestry Commission roads are open to cyclists and some are specifically signposted, like the 7 mile forest cycleway around Braeval near Aberfoyle. There is also safe cycling around Loch Katrine on roads owned by Strathclyde Water Board and closed to motorised traffic.

Education: Based near Pitlochry is the Institute for Earth Education (Blairchroisk Cottage, by Ballinluig), an environmental education network which runs a range of courses.

Health: Near Perth is the Centre for Natural Health (52 Main Street, Bridgend), offering a wide range of treatments and advice. The Institute for Complimentary Medicine public information number for the region is 073 832 249.

Food: Green omnivores may be interested in a guide called *A Taste of Venison from Tayside*, produced by Tayside Regional Industrial Office, which includes producers who cull wild deer herds or rear their stock organically. Wholefoods can be bought in Perth at the Highland Health Store (7 St. John's Street) and Healthy Options (35 South Street), and a limited selection in Dunkeld at Ibbetson's (Bridge Street).

If you want to eat out, there's the Osprey Hotel in Kingussie and Natural Choice in Stirling (5 Baker Street), both specialising in wholefood vegetarian cuisine. Restaurants offering vegetarian dishes on their menu include The Tuckshop at Carrbridge and Broughton's at Blair Drummond, Stirling.

Bookshops: Both Hatchards and John Smith in Stirling carry a small range of green-tinted titles, as do Waterstone's and Melven's in Perth.

Argyll

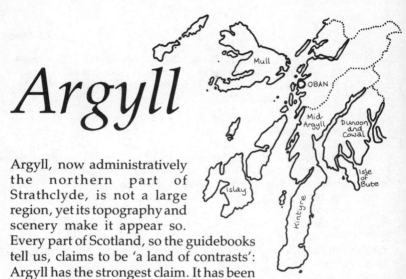

Argyll, now administratively the northern part of Strathclyde, is not a large region, yet its topography and scenery make it appear so.

Every part of Scotland, so the guidebooks tell us, claims to be 'a land of contrasts': Argyll has the strongest claim. It has been calculated that Argyll's coastline is, at more than 3,000 miles, longer than the distance from Glasgow to New York, but that coastline varies from the calm inner reaches of Loch Fyne and Loch Goil to the turbulent Gulf of Corrievreckan between Jura and Scarba with its notorious whirlpool.

More than a hundred islands add to the long coastline, from the large and easily-reached Mull, Islay and Jura, through the smaller and more intimate inhabited isles of Iona, Colonsay and Gigha, to mere skerries like the lighthouse island of Sanda off the Mull of Kintyre. The long sea lochs cutting deep into Argyll are augmented by the equally long freshwater Loch Awe, between them ensuring that wheeled traffic must be subservient to the lie of the land: the distance as the seagull flies from Glasgow to Campbeltown, for example, is little more than sixty miles, but take the A83 trunk road and you will clock up 134 miles before you reach your destination.

Fewer than 70,000 people live in Argyll (there are ten times as many sheep), but historically it has always been a vitally import-ant part of Scotland. Being so close to Ireland, this is the route by which stone age people entered the country, to be followed six millennia later by Saint Columba. The third century Kingdom of Dalriada had its headquarters at Dunadd, where tall stones still commemorate the site; Columba's influence can be seen in the many impressive stone crosses on which pagan and Christian symbols intermingle, most notably on the sacred island of Iona, where more than 60 of Scotland's monarchs are said to be buried.

Tourism is Argyll's second industry after hillfarming, and every other house offers bed and breakfast. Yet the brand of tourism on offer also varies considerably. Dunoon and Rothesay are the traditional holiday haunts of Glasgow folk; during the city's Fair Fortnight in July it is best to leave the Cowal resorts to their native throng. Inverary and Oban, though picturesque in their seaside settings, are not very different from most small Scottish towns dominated by tourism, while Campbeltown and Lochgilphead are working places with tourism more obviously tacked on. Walk the coast of Islay between Post Askaig and Port Ellen, however, or the south coast of Mull, and the views and the wind in your hair will remind you of what life is really all about.

Regional Tourist Offices: Oban, Mull and District Tourist Board, Boswell House, Argyll Square, Oban, Argyll PA34 4AN (Tel: 0631 63122); Mid Argyll, Kintyre and Islay Tourist Board, The Pier, Campbeltown, Argyll PA28 6EF (Tel: 0586 52056); Dunoon and Cowal Tourist Board, Information Centre, 7 Alexandra Parade, Dunoon, Argyll PA23 8AB (Tel: 0369 3755); Isle of Bute Tourist Board, The Pier, Rothesay, Isle of Bute PA20 9AQ (Tel: 0700 2151).

Ancient Sites: The region is rich in archaeological sites from standing stones to medieval chapels, but the highlight for many visitors will be the impressive series of Celtic carved stones to be found throughout Argyll, from the Campbeltown Market Cross of 1380 to the three mighty crosses near the abbey on Iona. The area around Loch Sween in the parish of Keills and Kilmory, and the Kilmartin area north of Lochgilphead, are particularly rich in Celtic art. Of a number of standing stones, the Stillaig Stones near Tighnabruaich are thought to be part of an ancient lunar observatory; this corner of Cowal is particularly rich in hillforts, cairns and standing stones (Dunoon and Cowal Tourist Organisation produces an excellent *Archaeology and History* leaflet: 40p from tourist information centres).

Iona is still a pilgrimage centre for many people, as it has been for the Gaels and their druids for centuries. It would be hard to imagine a more beautiful setting for the abbey church of St Mary, overlooking the blue waters of the Sound of Iona. Make a point of climbing the low hill of Dun I with its Well of Healing, and walking around the north and west coasts of the island to visit Traigh Bhan ('the white bay of the monks') and the Hermit's Cell. At the south end of this three-mile-long isle is the bay where St Columba is said to have landed, a beach of multi-coloured pebbles including the unique Iona marble.

Trees and Woodland: The Argyll Forest Park, straddling the north of the Cowal peninsula, was established in 1935, thus predating any of Britain's national parks by more than a decade. 165 miles of forest road winding through mature stands of pine, spruce and occasional hardwoods are open to walkers, and the Park also boasts several fine arboreta. The finest are the Kilmun Arboretum, overlooking the nuclear submarine base at Holy Loch, and the Younger Botanical Gardens a couple of miles further north at Benmore. Kilmun, a wild and invigorating arboretum set on a steep hillside, contains the largest collection of eucalyptus species in Britain, while the Benmore gardens are famous for their giant redwoods.

The gardens of Inverary Castle contain some impressive firs and cypresses, while nearby Crarae Woodland Garden is a beautiful setting for a collection of trees built up over the past eighty years. The Forestry Commission has been active (and fairly sympathetically so) in Knapdale; less sympathetically around Loch Awe where they thought nobody was looking. The Commission redeems itself a little north of Tobermory on Mull, where the Ardmore Forest Walk is varied and attractive.

Argyll also has some fine fragments of old native pinewood near Loch Tulla and along Glen Orchy, while the coastline supports what is left of the original cover of oak, ash, wych elm, wild cherry, birch, alder, rowan and hazel, with sallow, holly and the occasional guelder rose forming the shrub layer. This native woodland can be seen in three of the region's national nature reserves: Glasdrum at the head of Loch Creran, Taynish in Knapdale, and Glen Nant, east of Oban.

Wildlife: Because of its varied landscape, you can find an enormous range of habitat in Argyll: mountains supporting tundra and alpine flowers, raised bog and valley peatland, peat pools and lime-rich ponds, herb-rich grassland and rolling duneland — Tiree has the largest area of blown sand not colonised by rabbits in Britain. An interesting feature of the native deciduous woodlands of the region is the profusion of lichens encouraged by the moist westerly airstream; over 200 species may occur in a single woodland.

Golden eagles soar over the coastal cliffs, and peregrine, merlin, hen harrier, sparrowhawk, kestrel and buzzard are all abundant. The coasts support a rich marine life, and the Marine Biological Association runs the Dunstaffnage Research Laboratory and visitor centre near Oban. At Port Charlotte on Islay is the Islay Field Centre, where a variety of nature study courses is available.

Protected Areas: Of the region's four national nature reserves, three are the woodland sites mentioned above, of which Taynish is acknowledged to be an International Biosphere Site. The fourth reserve is Ben Lui, which straddles the border between this region and the Central Highlands. The mountain has a rich sub-arctic flora, including several saxifrages, roseroot, alpine saw-wort and the beautiful globeflower. Western Mull, Scarba and the adjacent islands, southern Jura, Knapdale and the Kyles of Bute have all been designated National Scenic Areas.

Access to the Countryside: Walking in most of Argyll is very rewarding and relatively easy, although care is needed in the mountains: Ben Lui and The Cobbler especially are surrounded by rocky precipices. The Forestry Commission and the local tourist boards produce some very good guides for walkers: the Commission's *Lorne Forest Walks* describes the Glen Dubh, Glen Nant and Beinn Lora walks; Dunoon and Cowal Tourist Board has four annotated maps covering its area; and the Isle of Bute Tourist Board has leaflets describing five waymarked 'Island Trails'. The West Highland Way long distance footpath nicks the far north-east corner of Argyll on its way from Milngavie to Fort William.

Museums: As you might expect, there are a number of rural heritage museums in Argyll, the most worthwhile of which are the Museum of Islay Life at Port Charlotte, the Easdale Folk Museum south of Oban, and Auchendrain near Inverary, the best of the bunch with its collection of reconstructed buildings giving a good idea of what Highland life might have been like in centuries past. The story of the Mull clearances is brought to life at the Old Byre Heritage Centre at Dervaig.

Communal Groups: Erraid is a small tidal island at Mull's south-western tip; over a century ago the Northern Lighthouse Board built a shore station here to service the lighthouse at Skerryvore, but now that the lighthouse is automatic the solid houses of Erraid are occupied by a largely self-sufficient community of ten people. Erraid is affiliated to the Findhorn Foundation (see 'Communal Groups' in the North-East Scotland section); they grow and catch much of their food (their garden is completely organic) and with advance notice they welcome visitors to participate in their community lifestyle.

A very different sort of community is The Iona Community, based partly on Iona and partly in Glasgow. Its impetus was the belief by George MacLeod, now a leading churchman, that the ecumenical message of the church was not reaching ordinary people, so the community set about the twofold task of rebuilding the abbey and its outbuildings as a retreat and holiday centre for city people, and sharing thoughts and deeds within a wide range of social concerns. Members of the community now live all over Britain, treating the abbey and the recently completed Centre for Reconciliation as a home from home when they visit for conferences and retreats.

Community Initiatives: The Mull Little Theatre at Dervaig is said, with its 37 seats, to be the smallest professionally run theatre in the world; there is also a pleasant restaurant, making an evening out an all-round entertainment.

Co-operatives: The region's only co-operative is Oban Crafts Ltd (see under 'Craft Workshops'), though Rothesay on Bute is the site of a brave experiment in community-owned and operated business. Bute Enterprises is a multi-functional trading company under whose umbrella come a pottery, a printing business, a landscaping business, and the provision of self-catering holiday accommodation.

Craft Workshops: Oban Crafts Ltd, a workers' co-operative, have a shop in Oban (Craigard Road) that sells a wide variety of their high quality work, and on the Isle of Seil you can see the art of woodturning at the Barn Craft Shop (North Cuan Croft, Cuan Ferry). For something a little more out of the ordinary, there's Grogport Rugs Organic Tannery (Grogport Old Manse, Carradale, Campbeltown), advertising a hand-tanning process that doesn't smell.

Nuclear and Anti-Nuclear: The shores of Loch Long are home to one of the largest collections of military paraphernalia in Europe. Holy Loch with its submarine base for American nuclear-capable submarines is the most notorious, the focus of anti-nuclear activity since the 'ban the bomb' marches of the 1960s. Coulport is a navy armaments depot, used to store Polaris warheads, while Loch Goil and upper Loch Long are both used as torpedo testing ranges.

The active anti-nuclear group Scotland Against Nuclear Dumping (SAND) has a strong presence in the region: SAND's secretariat is at 4 Fountainhead, Bunessan, Isle of Mull; its press office at Olrig, Clachan, Seil, by Oban. The Cowal Radiation Monitoring Group is based at Ryvoan, South Campbell Road, Inellan, Dunoon. Faslane is the site of Scotland's only full-time peace camp; they welcome like-minded visitors and you can contact them at Shandon, Helensburgh (Tel: 0436 820901).

Alternative Energy: At Cruachan on the northern shore of Loch Awe is the North of Scotland Hydro-Electric Board's 'hollow mountain', or pumped storage scheme as it is more accurately and prosaicly called. Here water is pumped up to a high-level holding reservoir when electricity demand is low, to drive massive turbines on the way back down to Loch Awe when demand is high. You can look round the visitor centre without advance notice, but you will need to book for the trip into the heart of the scheme, especially during the summer months.

At Portnahaven at the south-west tip of Islay is Britain's only wave power project, a thirty-foot high concrete chamber in a narrow gully known as an oscillating water column. The naturally tapering gully focuses the sea's energy before the waves enter the column; these force air out through the turbine. Air is sucked back through the turbine as the water level falls, making it doubly efficient. It is estimated that the wave generator can make electricity for around 7p per kilowatt hour.

Transport: All public transport in Argyll is covered by the excellent handbook *Getting Around the Highlands and Islands* (£2.50 from tourist information centres). With the many islands in the region, ferries are an important element in the public transport system: the two main operators are Caledonian MacBrayne Ltd (The Ferry Terminal, Gourock) and Western Ferries (Hunters Quay Terminal, Dunoon). The major bus company is Midland Scottish (Oban Travel Centre, Queens Park Place, Oban). For local services there is also the Gaelic Bus (Alexander MacConnacher and Son, Brecklet Garage, Ballachulish) for the Lorne and Lochaber area, while on Mull services are provided by Bowman's Coaches (Scallastle, Craignure) and I.K. Morrison (59 Rockfield Road, Tobermory). On Islay buses are run by B. Mundell Ltd (Bardaravine, Tarbert).

On the delightful island of Gigha, cycles can be hired at the Gigha Hotel and at the Post Office at Ardminish. On Islay you can hire bikes from MacAulay and Torrie (102 Frederick Crescent, Port Ellen) and from Islay Leisure (Bowmore Post Office, Bowmore). Bikes can usually be hired on the other islands too; ask at the local tourist information centre. On the mainland, bikes can be hired from Pier Stores in Carradale.

The Crinan Canal provides a short cut across the north end of Kintyre for fishing boats and small pleasure craft; it is operated by the British Waterways Board (Pier Square, Ardrisaig), who employ a ranger to look after wildlife and tourism interests.

Health: Most people in the region looking for alternative treatment go to Glasgow, though there are a few practitioners in the area. For details ring the Complementary Medicine Centre in Glasgow (Tel: 041 332 4924).

Food: Wholefoods still have to come to Argyll in a big way, but there are a few eating places for wholefood eaters and vegetarians. At Kilmelford near Oban is the Cuilfail Hotel, while at Lochgilphead you will find The Best Bistro in Argyll (Smithy Lane). The Argyll Hotel on Iona is green through and through, from its organic garden to its home-cooked wholefood meals. Jays Tea House in Oban (George Street) includes vegetarian meals on its menu alongside beefburgers and pizzas. Wholefoods can be bought in Oban from Millstone Wholefoods (15 High Street) and Oban Sesame (Esplanade); in Dunoon from Eco Grain and Health Store (50 Hillfoot Street); and in Campbeltown from Querstone Wholefoods (The Big Kiln).

Clyde Valley and Ayrshire

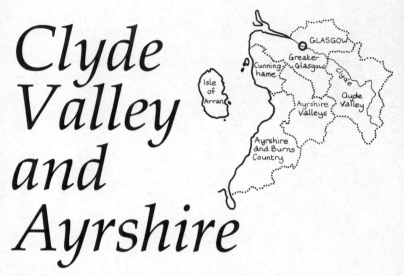

This compact area, now forming the southern half of the administrative region of Strathclyde, is dominated by the city of Glasgow. Yet it also contains large areas of barren moorland, forest and mountain, as well as some of Scotland's most dramatic riverscape.

Much of the Clyde Valley, together with the south Ayrshire coalfield, was transformed during the nineteenth century from a semi-feudal agricultural economy to a landscape dominated by slagheaps, railway sidings and factory chimneys. Heavy industry of every kind, from coalmining at Dalmellington to the recently modernised steelworks at Ravenscraig, is now in decline, quite possibly terminal decline, leading to an overdependence on state benefit

and companies looking to exploit cheap skilled labour.

These same areas, too often rundown and derelict, have in recent years been the location for some imaginative community and wildlife projects, and plans now afoot include a massive tree planting scheme to the east of Glasgow.

While the inland valleys have depended on agriculture and manufacturing, the region's coasts have long been a mecca for Glasgow and Edinburgh holidaymakers, with resorts from Largs to Girvan boasting a density of lodging houses and hotels to rival Bournemouth and Brighton. Even today the Magnum Leisure Centre at Irvine is Scotland's most popular tourist attraction, easily outstripping Edinburgh Castle.

Wherever you are in this area, even in central Glasgow, you are not far from the country. For a taste of the best that the region can offer, catch the bus to the Clachan of Campsie and climb the hill until you can see way over the Clyde valley; take the bus or train to Lanark and walk down to New Lanark and the impressive Falls of Clyde; walk along the rocky south Ayrshire coast with its magnificent views across to Ailsa Craig and Kintyre. Better still, take the ferry to mountainous Arran and climb the airy and exhilarating granite peak of Goatfell, where eagles and ravens fly above the ice-carved corries.

GLASGOW

One of the many suggestions about the origins of Glasgow's name is that it means 'the dear green place'. After years of being associated with the grime of heavy industry and the deprivation which accompanied both its growth and decline, Glasgow is currently pushing its new bright green image as hard as possible, a major highlight being the National Garden Festival held here in the summer of 1988. In 1990 Glasgow becomes European City of Culture, trying hard to put the Edinburgh Festival in the shade. The world is beginning to believe that Scotland's largest city is indeed miles better.

Glasgow was never as bad as its detractors averred, but it is extraordinary how a city which until the 1920s was so rich in life and livelihood could have become such an urban nightmare by the 1970s. Glasgow's post-war authorities took what seemed the easiest way out and tore the heart out of the metropolis, but in doing so they nearly destroyed its soul at the same time as creating squalid suburban dumping grounds for council tenants. The tower blocks and urban motorways remain in all their concrete glory, but Glasgow City Council now knows better. Though strapped for public funds, public and private groups are working together all over Glasgow on hundreds of community projects — housing refurbishment, small co-operative businesses, the shops and services that the people of Drumchapel and Easterhouse had been denied since they moved away from their city centre tenements.

Glasgow isn't an easy city for the short-term visitor to discover, though you can enjoy many of its treasures without knowing it well. But as well as the Burrell and the Willow Tearoom, take time to find some of the traditional tenements on Dumbarton Road which have recently been given a facelift (don't be afraid to climb the communal stairs and get a bird's eye view of the street and the back yard), climb one of the Hutchesontown tower blocks to see what it feels like when the lifts don't work, and don't miss the recently rebuilt underground with its unique slightly-stale breeze, pushed around the tunnels by the toytown trains.

Tourist Information Office: 35-39 St Vincent Place, Glasgow G1 2ER (Tel: 041 227 4887).

Wholefood Restaurants: Glasgow's greenest vegetarian restaurant, Basils, is run by a workers' co-operative at 184 Dumbarton Road. The food is simple but imaginative, and the prices very reasonable. Specialist diets can be catered for, and Basils is well worth going out of your way to find. The other restaurant to seek out is that at the Third Eye Centre (350 Sauchiehall Street: see under 'Museums and Galleries'); you walk through the bookshop and there it is on your right, serving a straightforward wholefood menu in a straightforward way. Ashoka is an Indian vegetarian restaurant in Berkeley Street, while other establishments catering passably for vegetarians and other healthy eaters include The Granary (82 Howard Street), The Ubiquitous Chip (12 Ashton Lane, off Byres Road: a favourite with richer students from the nearby university), and Babbity Bowster (16-18 Blackfriars Street: good puddings, live music on Sundays).

Wholefood Shops: Glasgow's two best wholefood shops are Grassroots (484 Great Western Road) and Evergreen (136 Nithsdale Row), both co-operatives carrying a wide choice of healthy foodstuffs. Running a close third is Forrest and Niven at 73 St Vincent Street. Roots and Fruits at 457 Great Western Road is known far and wide for good produce at reasonable prices, specialising in fresh organically grown fruit and vegetables. Banana Joe's at 715 Great Western Road has a smaller selection and operates a strictly non-South African policy.

Bookshops: When the Changes bookshop in West Princes Street closed in 1988 Glasgow lost its only radical bookshop, so now you have to make do with Waterstone's (132 Union Street) and John Smith (57 St Vincent Street) who both have small green sections, though Smith's is in the basement hemmed in by computer books. William Porteous (9 Royal Exchange Place) is good for maps and guides, and if you like rummaging through inviting secondhand book emporia you shouldn't miss Voltaire and Rousseau's book warehouse at 12-14 Otago Lane, near the university.

Museums: As well as the internationally known Hunterian, Kelvingrove and Burrell collections (the latter in its airy new building in Pollok Park, with delightful walks and a pleasant café), the Glasgow museums well worth visiting are the People's Palace, the Tenement House Museum, and the Kelvin Hall Transport Museum. The first two will between them give you some insight into Glasgow social history: the People's Palace on Glasgow Green has displays about many facets of the city's history, with an emphasis on labour history and women's rights, while the Tenement House (145 Buccleuch Street) shows how ordinary Glasgow folk lived until very recently. Miss Toward's tenement flat has not so much been restored as kept as it was when she died, box bed, stone hot water bottles and all. The recently opened Transport Museum, opposite the Kelvingrove Art Gallery, displays many of the tramcars which were once so commonplace on Glasgow's streets.

Shops and Crafts: Glasgow is a major shopping centre, with department stores and national chains a-plenty. There isn't much, however, which is particularly green-tinted. The massive new glass-and-steel shopping complex on the site of St Enoch Station is designed to rival the Pompidou Centre in Paris and is worth a visit, as is the pedestrianised Sauchiehall Street, the city's main shopping centre.

City Wildspaces: For its size, Glasgow has a larger proportion of greenspace than any other city in Europe. Mugdock Country Park to the north of Milngavie has woodlands and lochs, with a number of waymarked paths; the Visitor Centre at Craigend Stables is imaginatively laid out. Craigend is also the home of the Glasgow Urban Wildlife Group. Pollok Park, to the south of the city, is a favourite with Glaswegians, who enjoy walking through the wooded parkland (the Park also contains the well-known Burrell Collection and Pollok House). There are a number of green belt initiatives around the city, notably the Drumchapel Green Belt Project (52-54 Dunkenny Square, Drumchapel) and the Clydecalders Urban Fringe project (see under 'Community Initiatives' in the 'Rest of the Region' section). There are three community farms in the Glasgow area: Inverclyde Community Farm; Knowetop Community Farm, Castlehill Road, Castlehill, Dumbarton; and the Lamont Farm Project at Barrhill Road, Erskine. Glasgow Tree Lovers Society (82 Kirkcaldy Road, Maxwell Park, Glasgow G41 4LD) works to protect the city's trees.

Transport: Unlike most British cities, Glasgow still has a passable urban rail system, with real connections between the different overground and underground lines. The Strathclyde Transport rail timetable is available from stations and tourist information offices. Buses are in a sorrier state, with more than thirty companies operating a miscellany of frequently-changing services. They have, however, all got together to create a 'zonecard' system so that season ticket holders know roughly where they are. Strathclyde Buses, the heirs of the old city transport department, are still the largest operator, and details of all their services can be obtained from the dinky little turreted building behind the underground station in St Enoch Square.

Glasgow Cycling Campaign (53 Cochrane Street) is Glasgow's cycle campaigning group, while Glasgow For People (420 Sauchiehall Street) works to oppose massive road-building projects in the city in favour of public transport. Cycles can be hired from Dales Bicycles Ltd, 150 Dobbies Loan.

The Forth and Clyde and Monkland Canals run through the north of the city, and though they can no longer be used by long-distance waterborne traffic because of infilling for road and industrial schemes, they are managed by the British Waterways Board (Canal House, Applecross Street) for amenity purposes.

Energy Initiatives: Strathclyde University has a nationally important Energy Studies Unit. Heatwise Glasgow (2 Elliot Place, Finnieston, Glasgow G3 8EP) is part of a Britain-wide energy conservation campaign.

Communal Groups: Heruka (13 Kelvinside Terrace South) is a small ten-year-old community of practising Buddhists; Open Close (283 Roystonhill, Royston) is another small urban community, based on ecumenical Christian principles and working with local young people.

Community Initiatives: The Association of Community Technical Aid Associations has recently set up a Scottish office in Glasgow (58 Fox Street, Glasgow G1 4AU), which is compiling a database of community projects in the city and throughout Scotland. Bellarmine Environmental Community Resource Centre in Pollok (Bellarmine

Secondary School, 42 Cowglen Road) is the first of its kind in Scotland, and aims to encourage local people to take an active interest in their environment; it comprises a comprehensive library and resource centre.

Co-operatives: In recent years co-operatives and community businesses have been springing up all over the city, largely as a response to local economic conditions and the active support of the Scottish Co-operatives Development Committee, formed in 1977 to promote co-operative ways of working in the country. SCDC have their offices on the first floor of the Templeton Business Centre, for many years a carpet factory though it is modelled on the Doge's Palace in Venice. Today nearly 50 co-ops operate in the Glasgow area, working in a wide range of areas from business services to textiles. Of the specifically 'green' co-ops, the best-known include the wholefood wholesalers Green City, the Glasgow Wholefood Bakery at Dalmarnock, and the city's best wholefood shops and vegetarian restaurant.

Health: Glasgow's recently-founded Complementary Medicine Centre (17 Queens Crescent, St George's Cross; Tel: 041 332 4924) offers a range of treatments, including acupuncture, aromatherapy, homeopathy and remedial massage. Otherwise there are a number of practitioners of alternative healing working in the city; for details look out for the latest issue of the twice-yearly magazine *Connections*.

Local Directories: The nearest thing Glasgow has to a green directory is *Connections* (128 Byres Road, Glasgow G12 8TD), though the fortnightly listings magazine, *The List*, is strong on green-tinted happenings. *Green Fax* (17 Queen's Crescent), a Glasgow-based green information service, plans to publish its first directory early in 1990, which will cover the whole of Scotland but Glasgow in depth. The Greater Glasgow Tourist Board issues a useful bi-monthly *What's On* listings sheet.

THE REST OF THE REGION

Regional Tourist Offices: Clyde Valley Tourist Board, Horsemarket, Ladyacre Road, Lanark ML11 7LQ (Tel: 0555 2544); Cunninghame District Council, Tourist Information Centre, Largs, Ayrshire KA30 8BG (Tel: 0475 673765); Ayrshire and Burns Country Tourist Board, 39 Sandgate, Ayr KA7 1BG (Tel: 0292 284196); Ayrshire Valleys Tourist Board, 62 Bank Street, Kilmarnock, Ayrshire KA1 1ER (Tel: 0563 39090); Isle of Arran Tourist Board, The Pier, Brodick, Arran KA27 8AU (Tel: 0770 2140).

Ancient Sites: Arran has several stone circles, notably the stones at Machrie Moor, Farm Road and Auchagallon, all on the west coast around Machrie Bay. Coylton, near Ayr, is supposedly the original home of Old King Cole, the 'jolly auld sowl', while some eminent archaeologists aver that Greenan Castle, near Ayr, is the authentic site of Arthur's Camelot. Knockdolian Castle, above the Water of Girvan, is famous for its mermaid, who rises up from the water at night.

Trees and Woodland: The low-lying parts of the region were once thickly covered with deciduous forest, but woodland of beech, sycamore, elm, ash and oak is now almost entirely confined to copses and river banks. Notable deciduous woodlands include the Falls of Clyde reserve near Lanark and the Ayr Gorge woodland near Kilmarnock (leaflets available for both). The country parks at Culzean and at Brodick on Arran both include mature woodland, with particularly impressive oaks and beeches at the latter. There have recently been tentative proposals for a Central Scotland Forest, a large area of mixed woodland and open space to the east of the Glasgow built-up area.

Countryside: The Central Scotland Countryside Trust (Hillhouseridge Farm, Shotts) is an active co-ordinating organisation working to improve the countryside of central Scotland; they organise a programme of tree planting, woodland management and wildlife conservation.

Wildlife: The Clyde coast, even where heavy industry is still in evidence, is an important staging post for flocks of waders, while reserves such as Lochwinnoch and Loch Libo in Renfrewshire provide good cover for breeding waders and wildfowl. Unimproved meadowland in the region is scarce, but where reserves have been created, as at Auchalton and Feoch south of Ayr, rare plants such as gentian and butterfly and frog orchid thrive. In the south, where agriculture gives way to moorland and forest, roe deer, mountain hare and buzzard may be seen. The Clyde islands, from Cumbrae to Ailsa Craig, are a naturalist's haven. Ailsa is the region's premier seabird colony, while Arran has been described as a microcosm of Scottish wildlife habitats, lying as it does astride the highland boundary geological faultline. It is for marine life that Great Cumbrae is best known, where at Keppel the Marine Biological Station runs a museum and aquarium which are open to the public. Beach Park, Irvine, is the home of The Sea World Centre; as well as providing fairly conventional 'family entertainment', Sea World is also a centre for innovative educational and conservation projects.

At Foremount House, Kilbarchan in Renfrewshire is the Scottish Natural History Library; this is the largest collection in Scotland of material about Scottish natural history, and Foremount House is also the home of other organisations such as the Scottish Society for the

Protection of Wild Birds and the Society for the History of Natural History.

Protected Areas: Glen Diomhan on Arran, part of the North Arran National Scenic Area, is a national nature reserve, as are the Clyde Valley Woodlands and Braehead Moss in upper Clydesdale. The far south of the region falls within the Galloway Forest Park, though whether the Forestry Commission protects or decimates the landscape depends upon which conservationist you speak to.

Access to the Countryside: It is easy to find interesting and pleasant countryside walks in most parts of the region, though urban and industrial sprawl in the north tend to limit the choice. There are fifteen country parks in south Strathclyde, most of them grouped around Glasgow and offering a range of activities from pony trekking and putting greens to nature trails and woodland walks: a leaflet is available from the Scottish Countryside Commission (Battleby, Redgorton, Perth). Worthy of particular mention are the Chatelherault Country Park near Hamilton with its wooded gorge and William Adam lodge, Brodick Country Park on Arran, and Culzean Country Park, where as well as the spectacular castle there is a treetop walkway and an imaginative visitor centre. The most spectacular walk in the region is the riverside walk along the Clyde past Corra Linn and Bonnington Linn. A booklet called *Seventy Walks on Arran* is obtainable from the Arran Tourist Board at Brodick information centre, and a company called Afoot On Arran (Allandale Guest House, Brodick) organises full and half day guided walks.

Organic Initiatives: The organic revolution has still to hit the west of Scotland, but three smallholdings producing a range of organic vegetables are Auchenkyle near Troon, owned by the well-known naturopath Jan de Vries, the Egginton's at Back Road, Dailly, near Girvan, and Carol Freireich at 1 Burnside Cottages, Sundrum, by Ayr.

Museums: As well as Sea World and New Lanark (see under 'Wildlife' and 'Community Initiatives', two museums in the region well worth visiting are the National Maritime Museum at Irvine, where as well as a range of boats you can see a reconstructed turn-of-the-century tenement house, and the Isle of Arran Heritage Museum at Rosaburn, Brodick.

Community Initiatives: New Lanark, where a model community based on cotton spinning was founded in 1785, has again become the centre of an imaginative co-operative project. New Lanark is probably best known for its association with the nineteenth century social reformer Robert Owen, who chose the new village as one of the sites for his experiments in industrial democracy. After thriving for 150 years, the mill complex declined during the 1940s and 50s, until by the 1960s wholesale demolition had become almost inevitable. Then in 1974 the New Lanark Conservation Trust was formed, and the place started bustling again with builders and visitors. Already renovated housing has provided homes for 200 people, while the innovative visitor centre is due to be completed in 1990 — much of it, including the craft shop and restaurant, is already open. Much of the work at New Lanark has been carried out under community training programmes. New Lanark now receives more than 80,000 visitors each year.

The Clyde-Calders Urban Fringe Management Project (Motherwell Business Centre, 132 Coursington Road, Motherwell) was established in 1983 to provide support for projects to reclaim the derelict areas around towns in the Clyde valley; they are also involved in environmental education. The Newmilns and Greenholm area, eight miles east of Kilmarnock, is the site of one of Scotland's first 'rural regeneration projects', organised with the help of the Scottish Civic Trust: the aim is to develop the area's grassroots economic potential and to encourage community involvement in a range of conservation projects. East Kilbride has a very active Environmental Action Group (70 Kenilworth, Calderwood, East Kilbride) which organises a wide range of conservation projects in and around this 'new town'.

Co-operatives: Co-operatives in the region include Renfrew Home Crafts, a firm working in Scottish textiles, and Arran Recycling Company at Burnfoot, Whiting Bay.

Craft Workshops: Craft workshops are thinner on the ground here than in most parts of Scotland, but if you are visiting Arran then make a point of calling in on Arran Candlemakers (Spion Kop, between Lamlash and Whiting Bay), Kilmory Wood and Pottery Workshops (who use local hardwoods in their products), and the spinning and weaving centres at Bowd Cottage, Lochranza, and Silverbirch at Whiting Bay.

Nuclear and Anti-Nuclear: Hunterston 'B' nuclear power station is open to the public, but you must book ahead (Tel: 0294 823668): make sure you ask a few searching questions. Anti-nuclear groups in the area include ANNE (Arran for a Non-Nuclear Environment, Planetree Road End, Kings Cross, Whiting Bay), and the Ayrshire Radiation Monitoring Group (23 Montgomery Drive, Fairlie).

Alternative Energy: The National Engineering Centre at East Kilbride is the home of the National Wind Turbine Centre; here you can see a conventional 60kw wind generator and a small vertical axis turbine. Between Kilwinning and Dalry is Dalgarven Mill, the west of Scotland's only working watermill; there is a coffee room and shop, and the associated farm buildings are currently being restored as a rural heritage museum.

Transport: Information about ferries can be obtained from Caledonian MacBrayne (The Ferry Terminal, Gourock), and Transclyde rail timetables are available from all stations. Buses are more erratic; the main operator is Western Scottish Omnibuses (bus stations at Largs, Ayr, Kilmarnock and Troon). Paddle steamer enthusiasts should not miss the chance to travel on the Waverley, the world's only remaining sea-going paddle steamer; for details contact Waverley Excursions Ltd (Anderston Quay, Glasgow).

Bicycles can be hired at Prestwick (The Cycle Shop, 5 The Cross), and on Arran at Brodick Cycles (Roselynn, Brodick) and Whiting Bay Cycle Hire (The Jetty, Whiting Bay). Sustrans have worked with local authorities to create the Glasgow-Irvine Pedestrian and Cycle Route; an informative leaflet is available from local tourist information offices or from Greater Glasgow Tourist Board, Town Hall, Abbey Close, Paisley.

Health: Auchenkyle Healing Centre in Troon (Southwood Road; Tel: 0292 311414) is a natural health clinic offering a range of therapies including acupuncture, herbal medicine, osteopathy and homeopathy.

Food: For the most part healthy eating has still to come to the Clyde valley, but restaurants offering wholefood menus include The Honey Pot in Ayr (37 Beresford Terrace), Caprice, also in Ayr (Newmarket Street), The Garden Room at Sannox, Arran (Ingledene Hotel, Sannox), and The Good Food Shop and Tea Room in Brodick (Auchrannie Road). The Granary in Lanark (38 Wellgatehead) carries a small range of wholefoods, while Body Natural at 38 Wellgate sells natural cosmetics and cruelty-free products. Largs Health Food Store (29 Nelson Street, Largs) also carries a limited range of wholefoods, as does Nature's Way in Ayr (17 Carrick Street). Arran Provisions at The Old Mill, Lamlash, produce a wide range of tasty additive-free preserves, mustards and chutneys — well worth a visit.

Local Directories: There are no local green-tinted directories, but if you are staying on Arran, pick up a copy of the *Arran Banner*, the lively independent local newspaper.

Fife and the Lothians

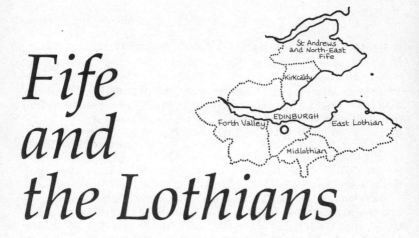

This, the smallest region in the *Green Guide* in terms of area but second largest — after the Clyde Valley — in terms of population, lies on the two sides of the deep Firth of Forth, and is bounded on the north by the Tay estuary and on the south by the rounded contours of the Lammermuir Hills. Today Fife and Lothian are linked by impressive road and rail bridges, but in past centuries each had a very distinctive character, much of it still discernible today. Even within the three districts of Lothian can be found barren moorland, rich farmland, the aftermath of a largely abandoned coalfield and, of course, Scotland's 'chief town' — Edinburgh.

Lothian once stretched as far south as the English border, but it now limits itself to the coastal lowlands within commuting distance of Edinburgh. East Lothian is noted for its rich red soil and buildings made from the same red sandstone; Haddington, the former county town, retains its spacious eighteenth-century layout. Just a few miles west, however, is the mining town of Tranent, with its rows of unimaginative council houses, and the proposed site of a new coal mine near Musselburgh. Between them the oil and

chemical industries mar the coastline of the upper Forth, where Grangemouth is home to one of Britain's largest petrochemical complexes.

'A beggar's mantle fringed with gold' is how Fife has been described, the difficult farming of the central hills being surrounded by charming fishing-and-tourist villages like Crail, Anstruther and Pittenweem, Buckhaven, Kinghorn and Culross. St Andrews, even golf apart, is an immensely appealing town — officially a 'city' — with its fine neo-Georgian building and wide streets. Its university, founded in 1412, is the oldest in Scotland and one of the oldest in Europe.

Wherever you are in the region, the sea and surrounding hills are always within sight, beckoning you to climb to the summit of the Pentlands or take a boat to the craggy islands of Inchkeith, the Bass Rock or the Isle of May. The silvery stone and pink pantile roofs of the little towns of Fife invite you to wander: start with Dunfermline and its fine Norman abbey, or Culross, a showpiece of National Trust-sponsored rehabilitation.

EDINBURGH

Edinburgh is a city of contradictions. It is the capital of Scotland (considered by many Scots the capital of the world), yet in British terms it is in most respects seen as a provincial city on a par with Liverpool or Newcastle. A higgeldy-piggeldy medieval town looks down on the Georgian elegance north of Princes Street, while the residents of the peripheral council housing schemes like Wester Hailes, Craigmillar and Muirhouse have good reason to curse the short-sighted city fathers who threw up acres of substandard housing in the 1950s. A financial centre second only to London and Zürich has been called 'the drugs and AIDS capital of Europe'.

Yet Edinburgh's reputation is as a genteel, cosmopolitan, art-loving city, rising like Rome from its seven hills to woo the world's tourists. And for those residents who can afford it, the city offers almost everything a city-dweller could desire: even craggy hills within easy reach of its bustling centre. In a detailed 1988 survey of British cities, Edinburgh was adjudged the best city in the country in which to live, bar none.

For the tourist, especially during festival time in August, a week spent in Edinburgh can be a satisfying and self-contained Scottish holiday in itself, though do take time to wander around the city as well as simply doing the sights. Though it is a tourist city, especially in the summer, Edinburgh is very much a working city too, which makes it doubly rewarding.

Tourist Information Office: Waverley Market, 3 Princes Street, Edinburgh EH2 2QP (Tel: 031 557 1700).

Wholefood Restaurants: Seeds (53 West Nicolson Street), a co-operative wholefood restaurant, is extremely good value; it tends to be crowded at main meal times but has a relaxed atmosphere and the menu is varied and imaginative. Hendersons (94 Hanover Street) has been around for a very long time; compared with other Edinburgh wholefood eating places it is rather overpriced but the dishes are tasty and the decor tasteful. Kalpna (2-3 St Patrick Square) is an excellent Indian vegetarian restaurant, no-smoking, and especially good value at lunchtime. The Cornerstone Cafe is an airy vegetarian cafe next door to the One World Shop at St John's Church on the corner of Princes Street and Lothian Road. Country Kitchen is a large restaurant at 4 South Charlotte Street; it offers basic wholefood dishes and a wide range of salads in a clean but rather soulless setting. Helios Fountain (7 Grassmarket) is a more alternative sort of place, using organic (biodynamically-grown when available) ingredients to create a simple menu; at Helios you also have the added advantage of a book and gift shop through which you walk to get to the cafe. Other Edinburgh eating places offering a reasonable range of wholefood and vegetarian dishes include the Gallery Cafe at the Gallery of Modern Art (Belford Road); The Round Table (31 Geoffrey Street); the Blue Parrot (49 St Stephen Street; lunch only; and Kris, an imaginative Malaysian restaurant in Raeburn Place. Be warned that most of these places are closed on Sundays, though Hendersons is open until 10.30 on other days.

Wholefood Shops: Real Foods (8 Brougham Place and 37 Broughton Street) has a good range at reasonable prices, with an impressive selection of organic fruit and vegetables. Roots (60 Newington Road) tends towards the packaged, while Nature's Gate (83 Clerk Street) stocks a range of macrobiotic ingredients. The Organic Vegetable Shop (Laurieston Place, Tollcross) sells produce from the Sprout Training Centre's market garden, an organic smallholding which has been established as part of a skills sharing project at the Royal Edinburgh Hospital: the range is small but quality and prices are very reasonable. 'Healthy living' shops have sprouted liberally in recent months, especially in the richer areas like Morningside and

Marchmont — in Argyle Place, Marchmont, for example, you will find a number of fruit and veg shops, many of them selling some organic produce.

Bookshops: Body and Soul (52 Hamilton Place) is Edinburgh's best 'green bookshop', with a wide range of titles from spirituality to vegetarian cookery; next door at 48a is Bookspeed, Scotland's alternative book distribution company. West and Wilde (25a Dundas Street) is a good radical bookshop, specialising in titles of particular interest to gays and lesbians. Both the One World Shop (see under 'craft shops') and Helios in the Grassmarket carry a good but limited range of green titles, while the Stockbridge Bookshop (26 North West Circus Place) is good for local books. The Scottish Ornithologists Club Bookshop (21 Regent Terrace) has everything you could ever want to read about birds and issues catalogues. Edinburgh has several large 'mainstream' bookshops, of which Thin's (53 South Bridge), Sheratt and Hughes (Princes Street, opposite the tourist information office) and Waterstone's (114 George Street) are all good for green-tinted titles. Of many secondhand bookshops, the best selection is to be found at McNaughtans' (3a Haddington Place).

Museums and Galleries: The 'big' Scottish museums are worth a visit: the National Museum of Antiquities (1 Queen Street) helps to explain Scottish history and prehistory, while the Royal Museum of Scotland (Chambers Street) is a beautiful building with the usual melée of engineering marvels and stuffed animals. On the Royal Mile are several interesting museums to visit, including the Museum of Childhood at 38 High Street, the Huntly House local history museum at 142 Canongate, and the recently-opened People's Story, a fascinating introduction to Edinburgh social history. Entrance to all these museums is free. Also worth visiting is the Water of Leith Heritage Centre at 24 Lanark Road.

Edinburgh is also home to a surprising number of art galleries. As well as the National Gallery of Scotland and the Royal Scottish Academy (both on The Mound) and the Scottish National Portrait Gallery (1 Queen Street), the two galleries in Market Street, the City Art Gallery and the Fruitmarket Gallery, are usually worth a visit. The Portfolio Gallery (43 Candlemaker Row) and the Stills Gallery (105 High Street) often have interesting photographic exhibitions, while Gallerie Mirage (46a Raeburn Place) displays an interesting collection of African and Third World goods, with some items for sale.

Shops and Crafts: Edinburgh's One World Shop is in the basement of St John's Church at the corner of Princes Street and Lothian Road — the entrance is at the back. New Mood at 33 Alva Street is the best of many selling cruelty-free cosmetics and natural remedies.

Edinburgh boasts a wide range of 'ethnic' shops including Azteca (12/14 Victoria Street) for Latin American crafts, and Out of Africa (Grassmarket) for African artefacts. The Byzantium Centre (9a Victoria Street) is housed in a converted church; here traders sell anything from second-hand books to hand-made children's clothes from open-plan stalls — there is a pleasant coffee shop upstairs. The Edinburgh Candles Shop at 42 Candlemaker Row sells everything you could want in the way of candles, including kits. Underneath the Arches in London Street sells interesting and different gifts. Ware On Earth (15 Howe Street) sells tasteful Mediterranean Pottery, with an art gallery in the back; opposite at Quercus you can see handmade ceramics, glassware and textiles.

City Wildspaces: Edinburgh has many open spaces and parkland walks: the Water of Leith Walkway from Balerno to Leith through Colinton Dell, Dean Village and Stockbridge is particularly attractive, while if you want more exhilaration and open views you might choose Arthur's Seat or Balerno Hill (The Scottish Wildlife Trust has established a visitor centre at the foot of the former). The Lothian Urban Wildlife Group is at Old Broughton Primary School, Broughton Road, Edinburgh EH7 4LD; they recently produced a detailed wildlife survey of the city and organise regular 'urban safaris'. Edinburgh Green Belt Initiative (2 Clerk Street, Loanhead) has produced a map and material about Edinburgh's green belt. Gorgie City Farm at 51 Gorgie Road is Edinburgh's city farm; it offers city people, especially children, a chance to see animals and crops at first hand and to join in with a range of activities. The recently-opened cafeteria and restaurant at Inverleith House in the Botanic Gardens are well worth a visit; tea on the terrace on a summer's afternoon is memorable.

Transport: When bus services were deregulated in 1988 there was a free-for-all in Edinburgh, and Princes Street was jammed with buses of all sorts and colours. Now that things have settled down a bit, Lothian Regional Transport and Eastern Scottish have emerged the clear winners. You still can't get a citywide bus map, but LRT do produce a useful series of route timetables which you can pick up from their office on Waverley Bridge, near the railway station. Eastern's minibus service is also reasonably good; both systems use the same bus stops, thank goodness. There are plans afoot for a new rapid transit scheme in the city, with two main routes, one north-south and the other east-west, using a combination of disused railways and new tunnels.

Spokes (St Martins Church, 232 Dalry Road) is Edinburgh's very active cycle campaigning group. Spokes has produced a detailed cycle route map of Edinburgh, and several leaflets about days out from Edinburgh by bike. They also produce a regular newssheet.

Cycles can be hired in Edinburgh from The Secondhand Bike Shop (31-33 Iona Street), Central Cycle Hire (13 Lochrin Terrace, Tollcross), and Sandy Gilchrist (1 Cadzow Place, London Road).

Energy Initiatives: Edinburgh Energy Centre at 17-19 Leith Street offers advice about energy conservation measures that can be taken by householders and businesses; they will be able to tell you about specific projects in the city. SCRAM (Scottish Campaign to resist the Nuclear Menace) at 11 Forth Street is a lively nationwide energy research and information service.

Co-operatives: The ten or so co-operatives in Edinburgh include Seeds Wholefood Café (see under 'Wholefood Restaurants') and The Magic Bean, a catering firm, Stramullion feminist publishers, and a Leith-based firm of river pilots.

Community Initiatives: Community Architecture (Scotland) Ltd has its office at 62 St Stephen Street, where the organisation works on feasibility studies and practical projects for involving local people in the design of their neighbourhoods. There are several community recycling schemes active in the city, including Papersave in Wester Hailes (90 Wester Hailes Road, EH14 3HR).

Education: The Centre for Human Ecology at Edinburgh University (15 Buccleuch Place, EH8 9LN) runs a programme of talks and workshops, and has an excellent environmental library which can be visited with advance notice. The Edinburgh Environment Centre in the old Drummond High School (Cochran Terrace, EH7 4QP) involves itself in a wide range of educational initiatives; it is also the home of IDEAS, the computer-based Information Database for Environmental Action in Scotland. The Dodos are an environmental theatre group which gives regular performances in and around the city: contact them at 43 Sandport Street.

Peace: The Peace and Justice Centre at St John's Church (corner of Princes Street and Lothian Road) and the Morningside Peace and Justice Centre are the places to connect with the city's active peace movement.

Health: Alva Natural Health Centre at 3b Randolph Place (Tel: 031 220 1987) offers a wide range of therapies, both physical and psychotherapeutic. Wellspring (13 Smith's Place; Tel: 031 553 6660/4988) is similar to the Alva Centre, offering space to a range of therapists and practitioners; it has been established longer than Alva and has a good reputation. The Stockbridge Health Centre, a National Health Service centre, offers several alternative therapies. The Salisbury Centre at 2 Salisbury Road offers a wide range of evening classes and weekend workshops in therapeutic, healing and creative skills.

Local Directories: By far the best guide to Edinburgh is the *Edinburgh Insight City Guide* (APA, 1989, £8.95); as well as being stunningly illustrated, the chapters on history, places and current affairs show the city as it really is and not just how the tourist industry would like it to be. *The List* is Central Scotland's green-tinted listings magazine, published every fortnight. Edinburgh Council of Social Services (Ainslie House, 11 St Colme Street) has produced an excellent free booklet called *Edinburgh Action*, which lists everything the budding Edinburgh activist might ever need, from charity shops and animal rights groups to health helplines and debt crisis centres. Two useful guides for those with particular needs are *Edinburgh for Under-Fives* (National Childbirth Trust, 1987, £2.95) and *Edinburgh and the Lothians for Disabled People* (Edinburgh Co-ordinating Committee for the Disabled, 1986, £1), while the Edinburgh Lesbian and Gay Centre at 58a Broughton Place can provide information about a wide range of gay issues.

THE REST OF THE REGION

Regional Tourist Offices: St Andrews and North East Fife Tourist Board, 2 Queens Gardens, St Andrews, Fife KY16 9TE (Tel: 0334 72021); Kirkcaldy District Council, Information Office, South Street, Leven, Fife KY8 4PF (Tel: 0333 29464); Forth Valley Tourist Board, Burgh Halls, The Cross, Linlithgow, West Lothian EH49 7AH (Tel: 0506 844600); East Lothian Tourist Board, Brunton Hall, Musselburgh EH21 6AE (Tel: 0368 63353).

Ancient Sites: There are impressive hill forts throughout the region, including Norrie's Law near Newburgh, where a great horde of Pictish silver was unearthed, Traprain Law in East Lothian, and East and West Lomond Hills near Falkland in central Fife. Maiden's Bower, a volcanic outcrop near East Lomond, possesses a natural hole pierced through the rock, one of many similar fertility sites where infertile women sought to heal themselves. Pictish symbol stones can be seen at Strathmiglo churchyard, Upper Largo churchyard and Crail old church; section 2 of Anthony Jackson's *The Pictish Trail* describes the Fife stones and how to find them. Wemyss Caves near East Wemyss is a series of sandstone caves which were inhabited in Pictish times; the school at Buckhaven houses an interpretative display, while the caves themselves contain a rich collection of early rock carving. Dunino Den, south of St Andrews, is a magical rock-cut well with a large celtic cross cut into the cliff face. Excavations at Soutra Hill on the edge of the Lammermuir Hills south-east of Edinburgh have revealed the site of a twelfth century hospital, where evidence of the early use of medicinal herbs has been discovered; visitors are welcome when the excavation is in process.

Trees and Woodland: This region is well-treed, but lacks the large-scale Forestry Commission planting of many other parts of Scotland. The mature pine trees in the John Muir Country Park (see under 'Access to the Countryside') are notable, as is the mixed Pressmennan Wood, south-west of Dunbar. Lothian is one of the few areas in Britain where Dutch elm disease has not devastated the landscape, thanks to a very stringent policy of regular annual tree surveys.

Countryside: The Pentland Hills provide stiff walks and fresh air a-plenty within easy reach of Edinburgh: the valleys of the Glencorse and Threipmore Reservoirs are well-frequented on sunny weekend afternoons. At Lochore Meadows, near Lochgelly in Fife, nearly a thousand acres of pithead dereliction have been restored to create a country park with a variety of landscapes and habitats. There are two 'community farms' in the region, where education is as important as agricultural economics: Livingston Mill Farm (Millfield, Livingston) and Balbirnie Farm (Balbirnie Park, Glenrothes). At East Wemyss on the Fife coast is the small but fascinating Wemyss Environmental Education Centre (Basement Suite, East Wemyss Primary School, East Wemyss). At Boghall Conservation Project (Bush Estate, Penicuik) is a nature trail which shows the relationships between agriculture and conservation.

Wildlife: The islands in the Forth estuary are well-known for their bird life: the Isle of May ranks with Fair Isle as one of Britain's leading migration centres. The Firth of Tay, forming Fife's northern coastline, is more gentle: here the tide recedes to reveal mudflats and sandbanks which are the haunt of geese and shelduck.

The hills to the south of Edinburgh, where agriculture gives way to moorland, are now mostly sheep run and grouse moor, though remnants of the original birch forest remain. The Pentland reservoirs (see under 'Access to the Countryside') provide winter roosts for thousands of greylag and pink-footed geese, whooper swans, wigeon and teal. The Royal Society for the Protection of Birds manages the Vane Farm Nature Centre at Kinross, where you can see a number of practical conservation measures in action.

Edinburgh Butterfly and Insect World (Melville Nurseries, Lasswade) operates on organic principles, and butterflies are also bred at the Kinross Tropical Butterfly House (Turfhill, Kinross).

Protected Areas: This is the only region in the *Guide* not to contain a National Scenic Area, and even nature reserves are few and far between, the most notable being the Isle of May, famous for its bird observatory established in 1934, and Tentsmuir in north-east Fife with its extensive dune system. St Abbs Head marine nature reserve near Eyemouth is one of Britain's few such reserves.

Access to the Countryside: Every summer the north-east Fife ranger service organises a series of guided walks: details can be obtained from local tourist information centres or the ranger service. East Lothian District Council (Council Buildings, Haddington) have produced a guide to the Yellowcraig Nature Trail to the west of North Berwick, while a guidebook available from the Regional Council Outdoor Education Department at Haddington describes several country and coastline walks around Dunbar. In this same area is the John Muir Country Park, named after the Scot whose campaigning led to the establishment of the great National Parks of America.

Organic Initiatives: A wide range of organically grown vegetables, fruit and herbs is available from Kirkhill Gardens at Arniston, near Gorebridge; East Broomhill Farm at Harburn, West Calder, offers a similar range. Organic Meat and Products (Scotland) Ltd at Jamesfield Farm, Newburgh, Fife, offers a wide range of 'naturally reared' meat.

Museums: The Scottish Agricultural Museum at Ingliston features amongst its exhibits the changing relationship between people and their animals from the early past to the present day, and the impact that past generations have had on the land. The Scottish Mining Museum at Newtongrange and its sister museum at Prestongrange tell the story of Scotland's coal industry. There are folk museums at St Andrews (the museum of St Andrews Preservation Trust) and at Ceres (Fife Folk Museum). Near Edinburgh, the Bo'ness Heritage Trust (86a North Street, Bo'ness) have recently opened for visitors the Birkhill Clay Mine and a reconstructed miner's home of the 1920s, and plan further developments to illustrate the industrial and social history of the Forth Valley.

The award-winning Scottish Fisheries Museum in Anstruther provides a record of Scotland's fishing trade and communities, while in Newburgh the Laing Museum has a displays featuring Scottish emigration and the Victorian self-help ethic of Samuel Smiles. The traditional crafts of coopering and wheelwrighting are on display at the Museum in Leven, while the Canal Museum at Linlithgow houses records, photographs and relics of the history and wildlife of the Union Canal.

The birthplace of the conservationist John Muir in Dunbar's High Street is open to the public.

Communal Groups: Monimail House near Cupar is a recently-established community which has restored a fifteenth century tower house; they have a large organic garden. They also work with disabled and underprivileged people.

Co-operatives: Co-operatives in Fife include Kingdom Joiners, manufacturers of garden furniture, and a Leven-based textile company. The Scottish Co-operatives Development Committee has a local office in Kirkcaldy (Ceres Chambers, 43a High Street) which will be able to supply up-to-date information.

Community Initiatives: West Calder Community Enterprise (Society Place, West Calder) is just one of a number of community-based recycling projects operating in the region. The Craigsfarm Community Development Project in the 'new town' of Livingston, established in 1966, has converted a range of old farm buildings to create a café, craft shop and furniture recycling service.

Craft Workshops: The Fife Craft Association has produced *Crafts in Fife* (available from tourist information offices) which lists craft workshops in the area and indicates those where you can see traditional skills being practiced, such as the Crail Pottery (75 Nethergate, Crail) and the Balbirnie Craft Centre in Glenrothes. The Swedish Weaving Shop (Back Wynd, Falkland) offers weaving and spinning tuition, and short courses in clay work are offered at Anne Lightwood Pottery and Porcelain in St Andrews (57a South Street).

Nuclear and Anti-Nuclear: Torness nuclear power station, opened in 1989, is what is known as an 'advanced gas-cooled reactor'. It was built despite strong local and national protest, which you can read about in the SCRAM booklet *Torness: From Folly to Fiasco*. It is sometimes possible to visit the power station with advance notice: contact the tourist information office for details. The Torness Action Group can be contacted via SCRAM at 11 Forth Street, Edinburgh.

Alternative Energy: Preston Mill (East Linton) is the oldest working water-driven meal mill in Scotland, although it is no longer in commercial use.

Transport: Bus routes are covered by Eastern Scottish Omnibuses (Dalkeith Bus Station, Eskbank Road, Dalkeith) and Lothian Region Transport (12 Queen Street, Edinburgh). Bikes can be hired in St Andrews from Gordon Christie (86 Market Street). Lothian Regional Council (Highways Department, 19 Market Street, Edinburgh) has produced an interesting and informative booklet of all the walkways and cycleways in the Lothians. Bo'ness and Kinneil Railway is a preserved line operated by volunteers; it carries visitors to the Birkhill Clay Mine. Timetable details are available from Bo'ness station, Union Street, Bo'ness.

The Union Canal crosses the region, and is managed by the British Waterways Board (Canal Office, Station Road, Broxburn), which has produced an attractive series of illustrated leaflets describing canalside walks.

Health: At Strathmiglo in Fife is the Westbank Healing Centre (Tel: 033 76 233), which has a long tradition of healing using touching and manipulation.

Food: In St Andrews, the Vine Leaf Restaurant (131 South Street) specialises in fresh seafood, local game and vegetarian dishes. Further down South Street at number 49 is The Merchant's House, and in Linlithgow The Howff (88 High Street) offers fresh food, home cooking and vegetarian meals. Elsewhere in the region, most restaurants claim to offer at least one vegetarian choice on the menu: these are listed in the *Catering Guide* published by Kirkcaldy District Council's Department of Leisure and Recreation. If you want to buy wholefoods, you'll either need to make a quick trip into Edinburgh or try local supermarkets.

Southern Scotland

The South of Scotland is too often that part which visitors rush through on their way to Edinburgh, Glasgow, and 'the real Scotland' supposedly only to be found further north. To rush through this varied and fascinating region is to miss a wealth of landscape and history largely free of the trappings of mass tourism.

Though the land flattens out in western Galloway and in the Merse of Berwickshire, this is primarily a region of high barren moorland; only four roads cross the lonely hills between Annandale in Dumfriesshire and the Tweed basin to

the east. Border battles and skirmishes in the 'debateable land' between England and Scotland made life difficult in earlier centuries, while the tight hold of estate owners over land and employment has often been maintained up to the present day.

Market towns dot the region, displaying an often incongruous mixture of traditional shops and chain stores, old-fashioned inns and modern hotels. The Borders towns have their mills and small electronics and food preparation units are scattered throughout the region, but the South of Scotland is rural through and through, as the farming pages of the local papers testify. Sheep, cattle and trees are the main crops, all overly dependent upon subsidies and the whim of politicians.

The South of Scotland is ideal if you really do want to get away from it all, and is one of the few parts of Scotland where you can walk all day through a variety of landscapes without meeting a soul. Climb Criffel or The Merrick on a clear day and you can see all the hills around from the English Lakes to the Mountains of Mourne: it will soon blow away your cobwebs and at least some of your worries.

Regional Tourist Offices: Dumfries and Galloway Tourist Board, Campbell House, Bankend Road, Dumfries DG1 4TH (Tel: 0387 50434); Scottish Borders Tourist Board, Municipal Buildings, High Street, Selkirk TD7 4JX (Tel: 0835 63435).

Ancient Sites: If you are within striking distance of the ongoing excavation at Whithorn Priory in Wigtownshire, it is well worth visiting this site where remains dating back to the first Christian settlement of the site have been unearthed. An imaginative visitor centre has been established, and many local people have found both employment and their town's past as they have become involved with 'the dig'. The lonely coasts of the Mull of Galloway are said to be the last home of the Picts, and there are enough rock carvings and 'cup and ring' marked stones in Galloway to keep the most dedicated antiquary happy for weeks on end. The south-west has several notable stone circles too, including the Twelve Apostles, north west of Dumfries, and the Torhouse circle west of Wigtown, one of the best preserved in Britain. And don't miss the eighth century Ruthwell Cross, one of the most magnificent of Anglian monuments with its runic and Latin inscriptions and intricate knotwork.

Merlin is said to be buried beside the River Tweed at Drumelzier, which is also the location of Scott's *The Lay of the Last Minstrel*. The Eildon Hills are full of prehistory and magic, for in the lee of the hillfort-topped summit Agricola founded the mighty stronghold of

Trimontium, 'the three hills', and nearby is the place where Thomas the Rhymer met the Fairy Queen: 'See ye not that bonny, bonny road which leads about the fernie brae? That is the road to fair elfland, where you and I this night maun gae . . .'

Trees and Woodland: The South of Scotland has more of its area under forestry than any other region in Britain, most of it conifer desert. Though the Forestry Commission has in recent years worked hard to make its plantations more visitor-friendly the simple fact is that forest monoculture is in general bad for soil, wildlife, people and local economy alike. Near Newton Stewart is the Kirroughtree Forest Garden; here you can enjoy quiet woodland walks and see the results of the planting of seeds of more than sixty tree species which have been grown from seed. Nearby at Gatehouse of Fleet is the Fleet Forest Walk; here the Forestry Commission is experimenting with mixed and deciduous woodland. In recent years there has been a growing interest in community-owned woodlands, and Borders Community Woodlands (The Steading, Blainslie, Galashiels — see also Tim Stead Furniture under 'Craft Workshops') organises tree planting and other educational projects. At Ancrum near Jedburgh is The Woodland Visitor Centre, opened in 1980, where you can see an informative exhibition about trees and woodland management. The Centre also has four well-marked woodland walks, an adventure playground for children, and a pleasant tea-room (with home baking).

Protected Areas: Four small areas of the region have been designated National Scenic Areas: the Fleet Valley around Gatehouse of Fleet; the East Stewartry Coast; Upper Tweeddale; and Leaderfoot and the Eildon Hills. Three of the region's eight national nature reserves have also been declared World Biosphere Reserves: these are the Silver Flowe wetland area in the shadow of The Merrick, the region's highest hill; the great granite hump of the Cairnsmore of Fleet; and the saltmarshes of Caerlaverock, famous for its pink-footed geese and oystercatchers.

Countryside: If you like wandering round gardens, there is many a treat in store in this region: you can choose from the National Trust for Scotland's 'training garden' at Threave, the Logan Botanic Garden near Portlogan on the Mull of Galloway, and Dawyck Botanical Gardens near Peebles. At Legerwood, between Earlston and Lauder, the regional council has joined with the Countryside Commission, the Scottish Landowners Federation and the National Farmers Union to create a 'farm trail', a nature trail with an accompanying booklet which provide an introduction to a mixed Borders farm which is doing its best to integrate wildlife and agricultural diversity. There are several farms in South-West Scotland that you can visit, too, but none of them organic. Blowplain Farm, Balmaclellan, near Castle Douglas is an 'open farm' where visitors are welcome to see how a Galloway hill farm works; they produce an attractive leaflet giving full details.

Wildlife: At Caerlaverock, south of Dumfries, is a fairytale castle with a moat and the Wildfowl Trust's premier Scottish nature reserve. Over 11,000 barnacle geese overwinter here, together with thousands of swans, ducks and waders. Lindean Reservoir, east of Selkirk (booklet available) is a good place to see waterfowl, and the occasional but not so welcome wild mink. At Monreith, near Port William in Wigtownshire, is The Shore Centre, a pioneering interpretative and activity centre; local schoolchildren use the centre to learn about shoreline ecology during termtime, but during the summer holidays visitors are welcome.

The Dumfries and Galloway RSPB have produced a useful guidebook, *Birdwatching in Dumfries and Galloway* (£4.95), which includes nearly thirty walks for birdwatchers as well as a mine of local wildlife information.

Access to the Countryside: In the wilder areas there is little to prevent you from walking where you want to (other than bogs and precipices), though it is hard going — and easy to get lost — in the large Forestry Commission plantations. The more popular paths, such as that across the Eildon Hills and the footpath alongside the River Tweed from Newton St Boswells to Maxton, have been sensitively restored by the regional council in the last couple of years. The 212-mile long Southern Upland Way from Portpatrick in Wigtownshire to Cockburnspath in Berwickshire is a real challenge for walkers, and includes some long and demanding stretches across wild and exposed moorland. The Countryside Commission for Scotland produces a general leaflet about the Way; the official guide is published in two volumes by the Ordnance Survey. Each volume comes complete with a detailed 1:50,000 map and costs £5.95. The Borders Regional Council Ranger Service (Planning Department, Regional Headquarters, Newtown St Boswells, Melrose TD6 0SA) has produced a series of *Countryside Walks* leaflets, and arranges a programme of guided walks. Similar walks, called 'Wigtownshire Wanderings' and 'Walk About Abit', are organised by Wigtown District Council (Technical Services Department, Church Street, Stranraer); the accompanying leaflets are full of interesting information about local history and wildlife.

Organic Initiatives: At Mid Shiels Farm near Hawick, cattle are reared organically for beef, while goats are reared organically at Cottars Farm, Hundalee, just south of Jedburgh. Organic oats and wheat are grown on the Gala Estate farms at Galashiels. The farm at

Locharthur Camphill Community (Beeswing, near Dumfries) is a small mixed organic farm, while there are several organic smallholdings in south-west Scotland, one of the most impressive of which is the walled gardens at Laurieston Hall, near Castle Douglas. The Local Herb Company at Culnoag Cottage, Sorbie in Wigtownshire produces a wide range of organically grown herbs.

Local Building Traditions: This is a country of white-painted low cottages and intricately-built whinstone town centres, to a large extent missed by urban redevelopers though kit bungalows mar the outskirts of most towns and villages. Border towns like Selkirk and Jedburgh are a pleasure to walk about in, as are the Galloway seaside settlements of Kirkcudbright, Wigtown and Portpatrick. Compared with towns in other areas, Dumfries is red rather than grey, being built largely from the more tractable local sandstone, while the famous Creetown granite has been used to face some of the more grandiose public buildings of Galloway. At Cove in Berwickshire is a 'historical trail' where you can visit the buildings and cellars used by fish curers as long as 400 years ago.

Museums: The Border Country Life Museum at Thirlestane Castle, Lauder, includes a number of reconstructed rooms where you can see the everyday things associated with such aspects of rural life as farming, fishing, labouring and craftworking, while at The Hirsel, Coldstream, the old farm and stables house an interesting collection of archaeological and historical exhibits. The Borders Museum Forum has produced an attractive *Museums Guide*, available from tourist information offices.

In the hills north of Dumfries is Wanlockhead, where the Museum of Scottish Lead Mining is worth a visit. Here you can go underground to look at the old workings, and see the restored beam engine. Galloway Farm Museum near New Galloway gives a good idea of what rural Galloway life was like until very recently, while in Ruthwell near Dumfries, where the first savings bank (later to become the TSB) was founded in 1810, you can visit the Savings Banks Museum.

Communal Groups: The South of Scotland is home to a number of well-established communal groups. In central Galloway is Laurieston Hall (Laurieston, Castle Douglas DG7 2NB), a huge Edwardian house with a walled garden, home to thirty people and an active 'visitor centre' which offers a wide range of week-long courses between Easter and October. Orchardton House, south of Castle Douglas, is a looser-knit and smaller community, while at Beeswing near Dumfries is the Locharthur Camphill Community, where able-bodied and handicapped people live and work together (see also under 'Organic Initiatives'). Edgewise at Coldstream in the Borders is a small community with particular interests in cycling (see under 'Transport') and permaculture, a sustainable type of organic agriculture. Samye Ling near Eskdalemuir is a renowned Tibetan Buddhist centre providing study, retreat and meditation facilities for Buddhists and non-Buddhists alike. The intricately carved and brightly painted temple stands out among the border hills, and as well as courses and retreats the centre also has an organic garden and craft workshops. Skirling House, Skirling, near Biggar has recently been opened as a small Buddhist community.

Community Initiatives: The Gracefield Arts Centre in Dumfries, opened in 1951 and still South-West Scotland's only public art gallery, is usually worth a visit, with two galleries showing a range of exhibitions.

Co-operatives: Sunrise Wholefoods in Dumfries (19 Glasgow Street) is a co-operative, as are the Jedburgh Press (who specialise in using recycled paper) and the Galloway Footwear Company (see 'Craft Workshops').

Craft Workshops: The South of Scotland is rich in craft industries, with small workshops at the end of many a sideroad as well as a few larger craft centres more on the beaten track. One such centre is the Homestead Craft Centre at The Hirsel, Coldstream, where you will find jewellery, pottery and leatherwork, together with Water Lily Weavers who produce exquisite handmade landscape rugs and wallhangings. The Sean Caer Craft Centre in Sanquhar (29 High Street) carries a wide range of useful local craft items, as does the Craft Centre and Fragrance Shop in Creetown (The Square), near Newton Stewart.

The Galloway Footwear Co-operative at Balmaclellan, north of Castle Douglas, makes a wide range of handmade shoes and clogs, while furniture-making from local pine and hardwoods can be seen at Tim Stead Furniture (The Steading, Blainslie, Galashiels) and Barrie Sinyard Furniture (Brook Cottage, Stobs, Hawick). The shop at the Priorwood Everlasting Flower Garden at Melrose sells an enormous range of dried flowers.

The Borders are famous the world over for their knitwear, though the industry is currently suffering a serious recession. The mill shops are the place to buy all-wool knitwear at very good prices: Hawick and Jedburgh are the main centres.

Borders Regional Council produces an annual *Crafts in the Scottish Borders* leaflet, while the Galloway Craft Guild has a regularly updated *Craft Trail*.

Nuclear and Anti-Nuclear: Chapelcross nuclear power station near Annan, one of Britain's earliest, was opened in 1958 to produce weapons-grade plutonium with electricity generation as an added bonus and sweetener. A tritium plant was opened here in 1980. Chapelcross Action Group is the local anti-nuclear group, and can be contacted at Bankhead Cottage, Canonbie. The region was badly affected by fallout from the Chernobyl explosion, providing added incentive for local monitoring groups to alert local people to the dangers of radiation; among such groups is the Radioactive Pollution Survey for Wigtownshire (Dhuloch Schoolhouse, Ervie, Stranraer DG9 0RE).

Alternative Energy: There are several large-scale hydropower schemes in Galloway on the Rivers Dee and Ken: the Tongland station near Kirkcudbright has a visitor centre, and the South of Scotland Electricity Board will pick you up and drop you back at Kirkcudbright Tourist Information Office in a little electric-powered minibus. There are also several small-scale hydro schemes in the area, like the one installed at Laurieston Hall (see under 'communal groups' which provides a large proportion of the communities electricity needs. In the picturesque village of New Abbey, south of Dumfries, is a restored traditional water-driven corn mill.

Transport: Public transport in the South of Scotland is not good, especially if you are travelling far. The two England-Scotland main railway lines traverse the region, but in general they don't stop! Only the local service between Carlisle and Glasgow through Dumfries is of any real use to the visitor. Bus services are slow and infrequent, but in the last year the decline has been reversed in some areas with the introduction of minibus services, often combined with postal deliveries (post buses).

The South of Scotland is good cycling country, and the Dumfries and Galloway Tourist Board produces a series of *Cycling Factsheets* giving suggested routes and general information. The pedal driven bicycle was invented by Kirkpatrick Macmillan of Keir Mill, near Penpont in Dumfriesshire, and in June 1990 an international cycling festival is planned for nearby Drumlanrig Castle. *New Cyclist* magazine, a bright and radical bi-monthly publication, is based in the Borders at The Lees Stables, Coldstream — they also hire bicycles (see also under 'Communal Groups').

Health: There are natural health centres in Dumfries (47 Castle Street; Tel: 0387 56644) and Castle Douglas (1 St Andrew Street; Tel: 0556 2982), which offer a range of therapies including remedial massage, acupuncture and psychotherapy. Alternative, a small shop in Dumfries's Queensbury Street, carries a wide range of herbal and homeopathic remedies, as well as cruelty-free cosmetics and toiletries, recycled paper products, some wholefoods and a small selection of books.

Food: Local specialities include trout and salmon (though most comes from fish farms rather than free-flowing rivers) and seafood (though remember that if you are near the Solway coast the Irish Sea is the most radioactive in the world). There is little in the way of good wholefood cookery in the restaurants of southern Scotland; most catering is either of the traditional three-cooked-meals-a-day variety or the deep-fat-and-microwaved instant meal. Opus in Dumfries (95 Queensberry Street) and The Herb Pot at Moffat (Dyemill, Sidmount Avenue) are among the few exceptions.

Finding a regular supplier of staple wholefoods can be hard in a farflung rural area like the Borders and the Lothians, so The Bean Machine (Barnhills Farmhouse, Denholm, Roxburghshire) is a wholefood-shop-on-wheels which visits towns and villages on a fortnightly cycle — an initiative which could usefully be copied elsewhere.

Bookshops: The best bookshop in the South of Scotland is in a warehouse on the northern outskirts of Dumfries. This is T.C. Farries (Irongray Industrial Estate), Scotland's largest suppliers of libraries and educational institutions as well as being open to the general public. Farries' have a particularly good selection of books of Scottish interest, and are also agents for Ordnance Survey maps and guides. Wigwam Bookshop in Lockerbie (42 High Street) has a surprising number of green-tinted titles for its size — well worth visiting.